First-Place Math

GRADE 4
TEACHER'S GUIDE

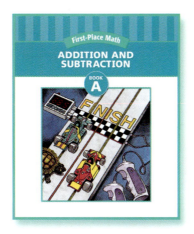

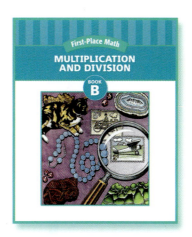

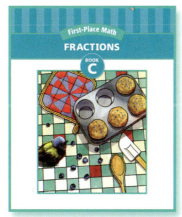

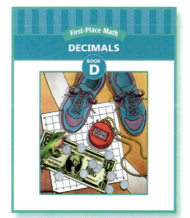

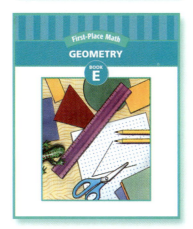

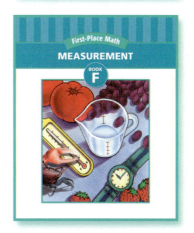

Orlando   Austin   Chicago   New York   Toronto   London   San Diego

Visit The Learning Site!
www.harcourtschool.com

CONSULTANT

Dr. Jennie M. Bennett Instructional Mathematics Supervisor, Houston Independent School District, Houston, Texas

REVIEWERS

Mary Beth Golombek
Teacher
Euclid, Ohio

Rosie G. Washington
Facilitator
Gary, Indiana

Richard Elsholz
Mathematics Consultant
Waterford School District
Waterford, Michigan

Mary K. Solberg
Facilitator
Math/Science Resource Center
Omaha Public Schools
Omaha, Nebraska

Copyright © by Harcourt, Inc.

All rights reserved. No part of this publication may be reproduced or transmitted in any form or by any means, electronic or mechanical, including photocopy, recording, or any information storage and retrieval system, without permission in writing from the publisher.

Requests for permission to make copies of any part of the work should be addressed to School Permissions and Copyrights, Harcourt, Inc., 6277 Sea Harbor Drive, Orlando, Florida 32887-6777. Fax: 407-345-2418.

HARCOURT and the Harcourt Logo are trademarks of Harcourt, Inc., registered in the United States of America and/or other jurisdictions.

Printed in the United States of America

Part Number 9997-41995-2

2 3 4 5 6 7 8 9 10   030   10 09 08 07 06 05 04 03 02

Contents

Introduction vi
Fourth Grade at a Glance..............................viii

Lesson Plans

Week 1–Book A
Addition and Subtraction

Week 1 Planner..T2–T3
DAY 1 ....T4–T7
Pretest...T5
   Adding 3-Digit Numbers
   More Addition
DAY 2 ....T8–T11
   Estimating Sums to the Hundreds
   Adding 4-Digit Numbers
   Problem Solving: Choose the Operation
   Problem Solving: Too Little Information
DAY 3 ....T12–T17
   Subtracting 3-Digit Numbers
   Subtracting Across Zeros
   Problem Solving: Use Estimation
   Problem Solving: Make a Table
DAY 4 ....T18–T21
   Subtracting 4-Digit Numbers
   Practice Adding and Subtracting
   Problem Solving: Make a Graph
   Problem Solving: Find a Pattern
DAY 5 ....T22–T27
   Practice Adding and Subtracting
   Add and Subtract
   Addition and Subtraction Review
   Home Connection
   Resources: Grid Paper and Number Lines
Posttest..T26

Week 2–Book B
Multiplication and Division

Week 2 Planner..T28–T29
DAY 1 ....T30–T35
Pretest..T31
   Facts Practice
   Multiplying 2-Digit Numbers
   Multiplying 3-Digit Numbers
   Multiplying 4-Digit Numbers
DAY 2 ....T36–T39
   Multiplying 2-Digit Numbers by
     2-Digit Numbers
   Problem Solving: Work Backwards
DAY 3 ....T40–T43
   Multiplying 3-Digit Numbers by
     2-Digit Numbers
   Problem Solving: Multi-Step Problems
DAY 4 ....T44–T49
   Dividing 2-Digit Numbers
   Dividing 3-Digit Numbers
   Checking Division
   Problem Solving: Choose the Operation
DAY 5 ....T50–T55
   Dividing by 2-Digit Divisors
   Practice Multiplying and Dividing
   Multiplication and Division Review
   Home Connection
   Resources: Grid Paper
Posttest..T55

Week 3–Book C
Fractions

Week 3 Planner..T56–T57
DAY 1 ....T58–T63
Pretest..T59
   Equivalent Fractions
   Simplest Form
DAY 2 ....T64–T69
   Mixed Numbers
   Adding Like Fractions
   Adding Like Mixed Numbers
   Problem Solving: Extra Information
   Problem Solving: Make a Graph
DAY 3 ....T70–T75
   Subtracting Like Fractions
   Subtracting Like Mixed Numbers
   Adding and Subtracting Mixed Numbers
   Problem Solving: Choose the Operation
   Problem Solving: Make a List

Contents

DAY 4 .... T76–T81
    Adding Like Mixed Numbers
    Subtracting Like Mixed Numbers
    Adding and Subtracting Mixed Numbers
    Adding Unlike Fractions
    Subtracting Unlike Fractions
    Problem Solving: Work Backwards

DAY 5 .... T82–T87
    Comparing Unlike Fractions
    Finding Parts of Sets
    Equivalent Fractions
    Fractions Review
    Home Connection
    Resources: Fraction Strips

Posttest T87

Week 4–Book D
Decimals

Week 4 Planner T88–T89
DAY 1 .... T90–T95
Pretest T91
    Comparing and Ordering Decimals
    Adding Decimals

DAY 2 .... T96–T101
    Adding Decimals
    Problem Solving: Extra Information
    Problem Solving: Too Little Information

DAY 3 .... T102–T107
    Subtracting Decimals
    Problem Solving: Make a Table
    Problem Solving: Multi-Step Problems
    Mixed Practice

DAY 4 .... T108–T113
    Subtracting Decimals
    Problem Solving: Guess and Check
    Mixed Practice

DAY 5 .... T114–T119
    Adding and Subtracting Money
    Decimals Review
    Home Connection
    Resources: Decimal Models

Posttest T119

Week 5–Book E
Geometry

Week 5 Planner T120–T121
DAY 1 .... T122–T125
Pretest T123
    Plane Figures
    Solid Figures

DAY 2 .... T126–T129
    Points, Lines, and Segments
    Parallel Lines and Intersecting Lines
    Rays and Angles
    Problem Solving: Multi-Step Problems

DAY 3 .... T130–T133
    Right Angles
    Problem Solving: Find a Pattern
    Mixed Review

DAY 4 .... T134–T139
    Congruent Figures
    Similar Figures
    Lines of Symmetry
    Problem Solving: Use Logic

DAY 5 .... T140–T145
    Ordered Pairs
    Geometry Review
    Home Connection
    Resources: Grid Paper

Posttest T144

Week 6–Book F
Measurement

Week 6 Planner T146–T147
DAY 1 .... T148–T153
Pretest T149
    Telling Time
    Estimating Time
    A.M. and P.M.
    Elapsed Time
    Calendar
    Degrees Fahrenheit
    Degrees Celsius

Contents

DAY 2 ....T154–T159
   Fractions of an Inch
   Estimating Feet, Yards, and Miles
   Measuring Millimeters and Centimeters
   Meters and Kilometers
   Problem Solving: Multi-Step Problems

DAY 3 ....T160–T163
   Perimeter
   Area
   Problem Solving: Make a List

DAY 4 ....T164–T169
   Cup, Pint, Quart, and Gallon
   Estimating Milliliters and Liters
   Volume
   Problem Solving: Guess and Check

DAY 5 ....T170–T174
   Estimating Ounces, Pounds, and Tons
   Estimating Grams and Kilograms
   Measurement Review
   Home Connection
   Resources: Grid Paper and Clock Faces

Posttest T174

More Manipulative Activities T176–T183
Base-Ten Blocks T176
Counters T177
Fraction Bars T178
Fraction Circles T179
Decimal Models T180
Pattern Blocks T181
Geoboards T182
Connecting Cubes T183

Alternate Planners T184–T207
3-Week Plan T184–T189
4-Week Plan T190–T197
5-Week Plan T198–T207

Welcome to First-Place Math!

First-Place Math is an instructional program that delivers direct instruction for math skills as well as data, problem solving, and vocabulary. In addition to the Teacher's Guide, *First-Place Math* includes the following components:

- **The six student books** include the core instruction for the program. Each book focuses on a particular topic in math and includes data and problem solving experiences for the student. The skills presented are intended to provide a review of the concepts covered in the most recent school year. The books may be used in their entirety or teachers may select pages to use based on results of the pretests.

- **The Practice Activities Book** contains extra practice related to the topics taught in the student books. The activities are designed to be independent and reinforce the learning of the day. The activities are suitable to be used at centers if the teacher chooses to separate the class into groups.

- **Games** provide entertaining reinforcement of the mathematics taught in each student book. The game cards can be combined to provide cumulative review and extend the problem sets for most games. The games are also appropriate for the teacher to use as center activities, if the teacher chooses to separate the class into groups.

- **The Daily Warm-Up Flip Chart** contains the *Number of the Day, Problem of the Day*, and *Quick Review* for each day. This allows the teacher to use these features without reproducing them.

- **The Assessment Book** provides a pretest and a posttest for each of the six student books. Student Record Forms are also included for each student book. The tests and record forms allow teachers to easily monitor student progress. The Assessment Book is the key to individualizing instruction to meet the individual needs of each student.

- **The Teacher's Guide** includes step-by-step instruction to guide the teacher through each day. The Teacher's Guide contains daily plans for six weeks of instruction. Alternate planners are included in a tabbed section at the back of the Teacher's Guide. Choose from the easy-to-use three-week, four-week, and five-week planners. More information about specific features of the Teacher's Guide follows on the next page.

The instruction for each day is divided into three easy-to-follow steps: Warm-Up Resources, Teach and Practice, and Extra Practice. The final day for each student book has a fourth step, Wrap Up and Assess. The instructional materials in the Teacher's Guide include the following key features:

- The **Pretest** may be given to students to determine which parts of the program they should complete. The Teacher's Guide contains correlation charts to tell which pages teach the specific skills on the pretests.
- In the **At-a-Glance** section, the teacher has quick access to the objectives for the day as well as the materials needed. Manipulatives are also listed in this section. With a quick look at the At-a-Glance section, the teacher can quickly gather the materials for the day and maximize instructional time.
- The **Warm-Up Resources** are given on the opening page of each day. Included are the *Number of the Day, Problem of the Day,* and a *Quick Review*. These activities allow the teacher to focus students' attention and prepare them for the upcoming lesson. These activities also appear in the Daily Warm-Up Flip Chart.
- **Vocabulary** words for the day are defined on the opening page of each day. This provides an easy reference, and allows the teacher to easily access words that will be taught.
- **Modeling the Math** gives detailed directions for using manipulatives to teach a particular concept. This feature is designed for the teacher who may not be familiar with modeling math concepts. Illustrations and text guide the teacher through the critical steps in modeling the concept. *Modeling the Math* also provides a basis for students to use manipulatives while they practice skills until they can work at the abstract level.
- **More Manipulative Activities** are referenced in the *Modeling the Math* section. These activities may be used to introduce students to a specific manipulative. These activities are designed to be fun and informally introduce students to the concepts that will be taught.
- **Reduced student pages** appear in the Teacher's Guide. This facilitates instruction, allowing the teacher to see the student pages while following the notes provided in the Teacher's Guide. The pages also contain answers to the exercises and problems, enabling teachers to check students' work quickly and easily.
- **Teaching Notes** appear below the student pages to guide the teacher through the pages. These notes include three sections: *Teach, Guided Practice,* and *Independent Practice*. The *Teach* section introduces the concept to be taught. The teacher is reminded to define the related vocabulary words. The teacher is also referred to the *Modeling the Math* feature if appropriate. The *Guided Practice* section allows the teacher to check whether students are able to go on to the independent assignment. In both sections, questions to help guide students' learning appear in bold type. Once the teacher determines that the students are ready to work independently, the exercises in the *Independent Practice* section should be assigned.
- **Extra Practice** appears as the last step in instruction each day. This includes a page from the **Practice Activities** book as well as a game on the final day for each student book. This step is optional and may be omitted if time does not allow for additional activities.
- **Wrap Up and Assess** guides the teacher through the *Review, Home Connection,* and *Posttest*. Correlation charts are provided for the *Review* and *Posttest*. The *Home Connection* informs parents about the skills taught in the student book, lists vocabulary taught, and provides a home activity to reinforce the skills.

First-Place Math

Grade 4

Skills at a Glance

Book A
Addition and Subtraction
- Add 3- and 4-digit numbers
- Subtract 3- and 4-digit numbers
- Subtract across zeros
- Use estimation
- Make a graph
- Make a table
- Find a pattern
- Too little information
- Choose the operation

Book B
Multiplication and Division
- Facts practice
- Multiply 2-, 3-, and 4-digit numbers
- Multiply by 2-digit numbers
- Divide 2-, and 3-digit numbers
- Divide by 2-digit divisors
- Check division
- Choose the operation
- Work backwards
- Multi-step problems

Book C
Fractions
- Equivalent fractions
- Simplest form
- Mixed numbers
- Add like fractions and mixed numbers
- Subtract like fractions and mixed numbers
- Add and subtract unlike fractions with models
- Compare unlike fractions with models
- Make a graph
- Work backwards
- Make a list
- Extra information
- Choose the operation

Book D
Decimals
- Compare and order decimals
- Add decimals through hundredths
- Subtract decimals through hundredths
- Add and subtract money
- Multi-step problems
- Extra information
- Too little information
- Make a table
- Guess and check

Book E
Geometry
- Plane and solid figures
- Points, lines, and segments
- Parallel and intersecting lines
- Rays and angles
- Right angles
- Congruent and similar figures
- Lines of symmetry
- Ordered pairs
- Find a pattern
- Use logic
- Multi-step problems

Book F
Measurement
- Time and calendar
- Customary and metric measurement
- Perimeter, area, and volume
- Guess and check
- Make a list
- Multi-step problems

Problem Solving Skills at a Glance

Book A
Addition and Subtraction
- Choose the Operation
- Too Little Information
- Use Estimation
- Make a Table
- Make a Graph
- Find a Pattern

Book B
Multiplication and Division
- Work Backwards
- Multi-Step Problems
- Choose the Operation

Book C
Fractions
- Extra Information
- Make a Graph
- Choose the Operation
- Make a List
- Work Backwards

Book D
Decimals
- Extra Information
- Too Little Information
- Make a Table
- Multi-Step Problems
- Guess and Check

Book E
Geometry
- Multi-Step Problems
- Find a Pattern
- Use Logic

Book F
Measurement
- Multi-Step Problems
- Make a List
- Guess and check

Manipulatives at a Glance

Manipulatives	Skill	Page
Base-Ten Blocks	Adding 3-Digit Numbers	A1
Base-Ten Blocks	3-Digit Subtraction	A8
Counters	Facts Practice	B1
Base-Ten Blocks	Multiplying 2-Digit Numbers	B2
Base-Ten Blocks	Dividing 2-Digit Numbers	B11
Fraction Bars	Equivalent Fractions	C1
Fraction Circles	Comparing Unlike Fractions	C24
Decimal Models	Comparing and Ordering Decimals	D1
Pattern Blocks	Lines of Symmetry	E15
Geoboard	Perimeter	F14
Connecting Cubes	Volume	F22

Week 1 Planner

OBJECTIVES
SKILLS
- To add 3-digit and 4-digit numbers
- To estimate sums to hundreds
- To subtract 3-digit and 4-digit numbers
- To subtract across zeros
- To practice addition and subtraction

	DAY 1 pages T4–T7	**DAY 2** pages T8–T11
1 Warm-Up	**WARM-UP RESOURCES** Number of the Day, p. 1 Problem of the Day, p. 1 Quick Review, p. 1	**WARM-UP RESOURCES** Number of the Day, p. 2 Problem of the Day, p. 2 Quick Review, p. 2
2 Teach and Practice	Adding 3-Digit Numbers, p. A1 More Addition, p. A2	Estimating Sums to the Hundreds, p. A3 Adding 4-Digit Numbers, pp. A4–A5 Choose the Operation, p. A6 Too Little Information, p. A7
3 Extra Practice	Fast Facts, p. P1	Use the Code, p. P2
4 Wrap Up and Assess	**PRETEST** Book A Pretest, pp. 1–2 　Assess knowledge of addition, subtraction, and problem solving	

First-Place Math

Addition and Subtraction

OBJECTIVES (CONTINUED)
PROBLEM SOLVING
- To solve problems by choosing the operation
- To identify what information is missing that is needed to solve a problem
- To solve problems using estimation
- To make a table to solve problems
- To make a graph to solve problems
- To find a pattern

DAY 3
pages T12–T17

WARM-UP RESOURCES
Number of the Day, p. 3
Problem of the Day, p. 3
Quick Review, p. 3

3-Digit Subtraction, p. A8
Subtracting 3-Digit Numbers, p. A9
Subtracting Across Zeros, p. A10
Use Estimation, p. A11
Make a Table, p. A12

Cross-number Puzzle, p. P3

DAY 4
pages T18–T21

WARM-UP RESOURCES
Number of the Day, p. 4
Problem of the Day, p. 4
Quick Review, p. 4

Subtracting 4-Digit Numbers, p. A13
Practice Adding and Subtracting, p. A14
Make a Graph, p. A15
Find a Pattern, p. A16

What's Missing?, p. P4

DAY 5
pages T22–T27

WARM-UP RESOURCES
Number of the Day, p. 5
Problem of the Day, p. 5
Quick Review, p. 5

Practice Adding and Subtracting, p. A17
Add and Subtract, Start to Finish, p. A18

The Sum of 1,089, p. P5
Facts Practice, p. P6

Game: *Zoom*

WRAP UP
Review, p. A19
Home Connection, p. A20

TEST
Book A Test, pp. 3–4
  Assess knowledge of addition, subtraction, and problem solving

Book A T3

Week 1

Addition and Subtraction

DAY 1 At a Glance

Objectives
- To assess knowledge of addition and subtraction
- To add 3-digit numbers

1 Warm-Up Resources
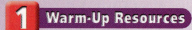
- Number of the Day
- Problem of the Day
- Quick Review

Book A Pretest, pp. 1–2

2 Teach and Practice

Book A • Addition and Subtraction, pp. A1–A2

Manipulatives: Base-ten blocks

3 Extra Practice

Practice Activities, p. P1

---

1 Warm-Up Resources

Have students work the following problems. Discuss their strategies and solutions.

Number of the Day

Write any 3-digit number. Then work with three other students and write the four 3-digit numbers in order from least to greatest. **Answers will vary.**

Problem of the Day

Find the missing digits.

```
  ■ 3 5        ■ 2 4
+   7 ■ 8    + 5 ■ 6
  ─────        ─────
  1 3 1        9 8
```

Quick Review

1. 18 + 28   **46**
2. 40 − 23   **17**
3. 71 − 37   **34**
4. 87 + 13   **100**

Vocabulary

addend — any of the numbers that are added (p. A1)

sum — the answer to an addition problem (p. A1)

regroup — to exchange amounts of equal value to rename a number (p. A1)

T4 First-Place Math

Pretest

Have students complete the Pretest (Assessment, pp. 1–2) for Book A • Addition and Subtraction.

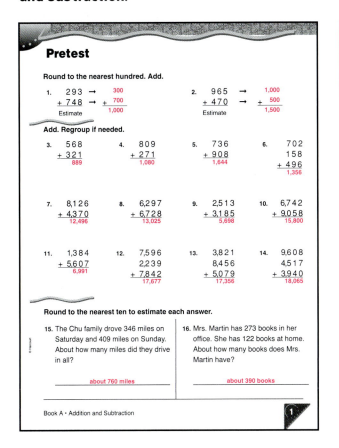
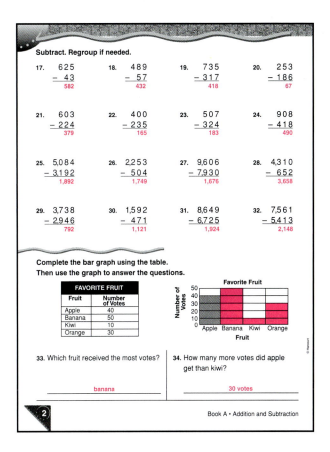

Pretest Items	Skill	Review
1–2	Estimate Sums to the Hundreds	A3
3–6	Add 3-Digit Numbers	A1–A2
7–14	Add 4-Digit Numbers	A4–A5
15–16	Use Estimation	A11
17–20	3-Digit Subtraction	A8–A9
21–24	Subtract Across Zeros	A10
25–32	Subtract 4-Digit Numbers	A13
33–34	Make a Graph	A15

Check What Students Know
If a student answers an item incorrectly, refer to the "Review" column to determine where the related skill is taught. You may wish to record students' results on their record forms. (**Assessment**, p. 25)

2 Teach and Practice

For an introductory activity using base-ten blocks, see *More Manipulative Activities*, p. T176.

Modeling the Math

Use base-ten blocks to model 368 + 235. Then have students use models to work similar problems.

1. Show a group of 3 hundreds, 6 tens, and 8 ones, and another with 2 hundreds, 3 tens, and 5 ones.

```
  3 6 8
+ 2 3 5
```

2. Add the ones.

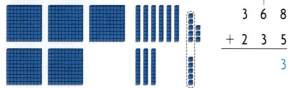

```
    1
  3 6 8
+ 2 3 5
      3
```

8 ones + 5 ones = 13 ones

Regroup 13 ones as 1 ten 3 ones.

3. Add the tens.

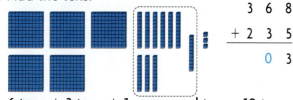

```
  1 1
  3 6 8
+ 2 3 5
    0 3
```

6 tens + 3 tens + 1 regrouped ten = 10 tens

Regroup 10 tens as 1 hundred 0 tens.

4. Add the hundreds.

```
  1 1
  3 6 8
+ 2 3 5
  6 0 3
```

3 hundreds + 2 hundreds + 1 regrouped hundred = 6 hundreds

So, 368 + 235 = 603.

Teach Page A1 Define the vocabulary words for p. A1. Use base-ten blocks to model the example problem as described in the *Modeling the Math*. First, model each addend. Then combine the blocks in each place-value position starting with the ones. Record any regrouping that is necessary. **Why was a small 1 above the tens column and a 3 in the ones column used to record the sum of the ones?** 8 ones + 5 ones = 13 ones. Regroup 13 ones as 1 ten 3 ones. Record the 1 ten above the tens column and the 3 ones in the ones column.

Guided Practice You may wish to have students model Exercises 1 and 2. Check students' answers. **When do you need to regroup?** when the sum of the digits in a place-value position is 10 or greater

Independent Practice Assign Exercises 3–16.

● You may wish to also teach p. A2 before students work independently.

First-Place Math

3 Extra Practice

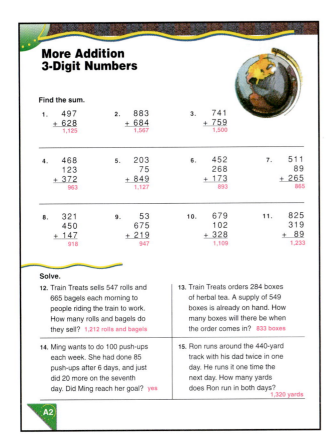

After students complete p. A2, you may wish to assign **Practice Activities**, p. P1.

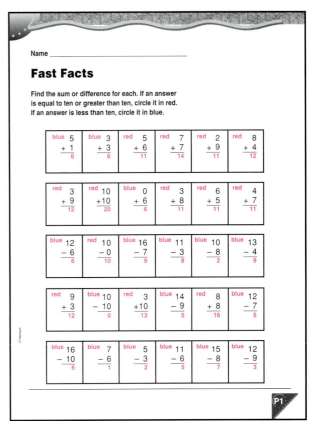

Teach Page A2 Use base-ten blocks to model Exercise 1. Show 4 hundreds, 9 tens, and 7 ones. Then show 6 hundreds, 2 tens, and 8 ones. Add the ones, the tens, and the hundreds. Show how regrouping is recorded. **Did you need to regroup hundreds? Explain.** Yes; 4 hundreds + 6 hundreds + 1 regrouped hundred = 11 hundreds, or 1 thousand 1 hundred.

Guided Practice Have students complete Exercise 4. Check students' answers. **How is adding three addends similar to adding two addends?** You line up "like" place-values, begin adding with the ones, and add from right to left.

Independent Practice Assign Exercises 2–3 and 5–15.

Week 1

Addition and Subtraction

DAY 2 At a Glance

Objectives
- To estimate sums to hundreds
- To add 4-digit numbers

Problem Solving
- To solve problems by choosing the operation
- To identify what information is missing that is needed to solve a problem

1 Warm-Up Resources
- Number of the Day
- Problem of the Day
- Quick Review

2 Teach and Practice

Book A • Addition and Subtraction, pp. A3–A7

3 Extra Practice

Practice Activities, p. P2

T8 First-Place Math

---

1 Warm-Up Resources

Have students work the following problems. Discuss their strategies and solutions.

Number of the Day
Add the digits in your ZIP code. Write a number sentence for your addition problem. Answers will vary.

Problem of the Day
Lucky's leash is 10 feet long. Buddy's leash is 5 feet longer than Spot's leash. Spot's leash is twice as long as Lucky's. How long is each dog's leash? Lucky's, 10 ft; Spot's, 20 ft; Buddy's, 25 ft

Quick Review
1. 460 + 28 488
2. 804 + 257 1,061
3. 175 + 250 425
4. 355 + 147 502

Vocabulary

estimate — to find an answer that is close to the exact answer (p. A3)

round — to replace a number with another number that tells about how many (p. A3)

2 Teach and Practice

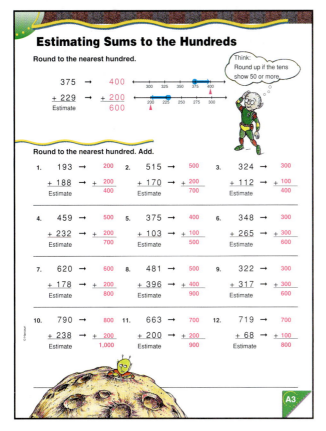

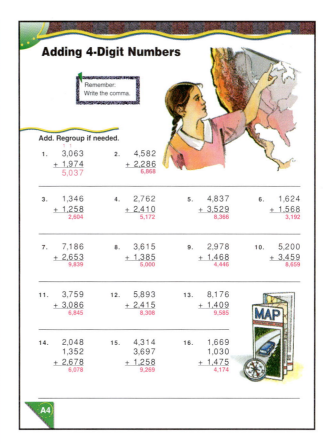

Teach Page A3 Define the vocabulary words for p. A3. Use number lines to model the example problem. Students may use the blank number lines on p. A21. Review the rules for rounding numbers to the nearest hundred. Remind students that when the tens digit is 5 or greater, you round to the next hundred. **Which digit should you look at when rounding to the nearest hundred?** the tens digit

Guided Practice Have students complete Exercise 1. Check students' answers. **Will the actual sum be greater than or less than 400? Explain how you know.** Less than; since each addend is less than 200, the sum will be less than 400.

Independent Practice Assign Exercises 2–12.

- After students complete p. A3, continue instruction to teach p. A4.

Teach Page A4 Direct students to look at Exercise 1. **How is adding 4-digit numbers different from adding 3-digit numbers?** Possible answer: With 4-digit numbers, you will have thousands as well as hundreds, tens, and ones to add, and with 3-digit numbers, you will only have hundreds, tens, and ones to add. **If you are adding the hundreds, when would you need to regroup?** when there are ten or more hundreds

Guided Practice Have students solve Exercise 2. Check students' answers. **In what place did you need to regroup?** the tens place

Independent Practice Assign Exercises 3–16.

- You may wish to also teach p. A5 before students work independently.

Book A T9

2 Teach and Practice continued

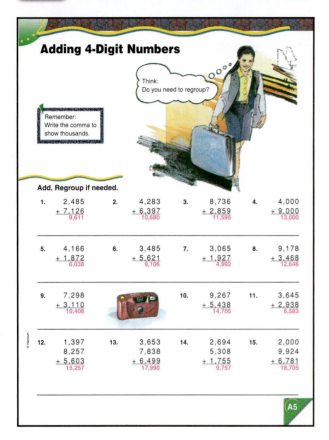

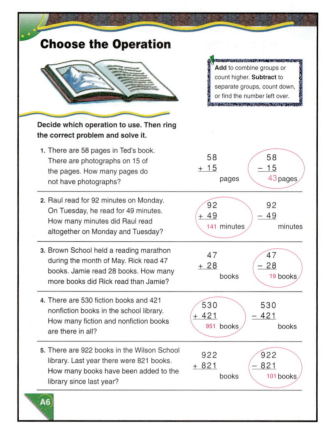

Teach Page A5 Use grid paper to record Exercise 1. Grid paper is found on p. A21. Explain how to line up like place-values. Add step-by-step, beginning with the ones. **How is adding 4-digit numbers like adding 3-digit numbers?** For both, you line up like place-values and add from right to left.

Guided Practice Have students complete Exercise 2. Check students' answers. **How can you use estimation to check if your answer is reasonable?** Possible answer: Round each addend to the nearest thousand. $4,000 + 6,000 = 10,000$; Since 10,680 is close to 10,000, the answer is reasonable.

Independent Practice Assign Exercises 3–15. Note that students may use mental math for Exercise 4.

- After students complete p. A5, continue instruction to teach p. A6.

Teach Page A6 Direct students' attention to Problem 1. **How do you know whether to add or subtract to solve this problem?** Since you know the total number of pages and the number of those pages that have photographs, you would subtract to find the number of pages left in the book that do not have photographs.

Guided Practice Have students solve Problem 2. Check students' answers. **What operation did you use to solve the problem? Explain.** Addition; since you want to find the total number of minutes Raul read on Monday and Tuesday, you add.

Independent Practice Assign Problems 3–5.

- You may wish to also teach p. A7 before students work independently.

T10 First-Place Math

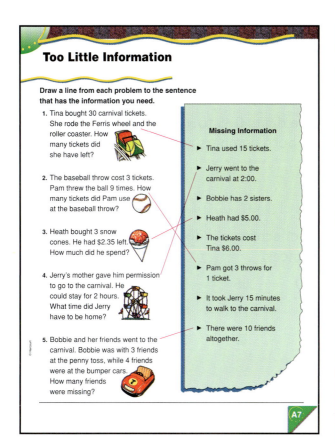

Teach Page A7 Read Problem 1 aloud. **Why can't you solve this problem with the information given?** You need to know how many tickets Tina used on the Ferris wheel and roller coaster. Help students find the missing information in the column on the right.

Guided Practice Have students find the information needed to solve Problem 2. Check students' answers. **If Pam decided to throw 3 more balls, how many more tickets would she need?** 1 ticket

Independent Practice Assign Problems 3–5.

After students complete p. A7, you may wish to assign **Practice Activities**, p. P2.

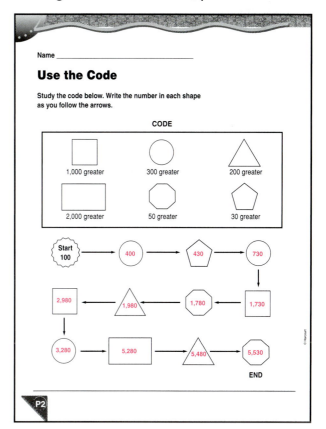

Book A T11

Week 1

Addition and Subtraction

DAY 3 At a Glance

Objectives
- To subtract 3-digit numbers
- To subtract across zeros

Problem Solving
- To solve problems using estimation
- To make a table to solve problems

1 Warm-Up Resources
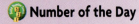 Number of the Day
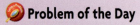 Problem of the Day
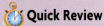 Quick Review

2 Teach and Practice

Book A • Addition and Subtraction pp. A8–A12

Manipulatives: Base-ten blocks

3 Extra Practice

Practice Activities, p. P3

T12 First-Place Math

---

1 Warm-Up Resources

Have students work the following problems. Discuss their strategies and solutions.

Number of the Day
Use the digits 0–5 to write a subtraction problem where both numbers and the difference each have 2 digits. **Answers will vary.**

Problem of the Day
Subtract across and down. Find the missing differences.

90 − 56 = ■ **34**

62 − 29 = ■ **33**

■ − ■ = ■ **1**

28   **27**

Quick Review
1. Add: 412 + 259 **671**
2. Subtract: 74 − 28 **46**
3. 500 can be written as 4 hundreds and how many tens? **10**
4. Round 114, 368, and 924 each to the nearest hundred. **100; 400; 900**

Vocabulary

difference	the answer to a subtraction problem (p. A8)
table	a way to organize data using rows and columns (p. A12)

2 Teach and Practice

For an introductory activity using base-ten blocks, see *More Manipulative Activities*, p. T176.

Modeling the Math

Use base-ten blocks to model 462 − 79. Then have students use models to work similar problems.

1. Show a group of 4 hundreds, 6 tens, and 2 ones.

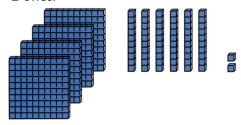

2. Try to subtract 9 ones. Since there are not enough ones, regroup 1 ten as 10 ones. Subtract 9 ones.

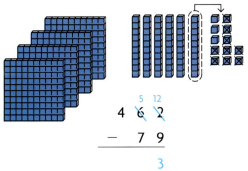

3. Try to subtract 7 tens. Since there are not enough tens, regroup 1 hundred as 10 tens. Subtract 7 tens. Subtract 0 hundreds.

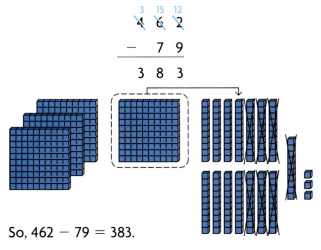

So, 462 − 79 = 383.

Teach Page A8 Define the vocabulary word for p. A8. Use base-ten blocks to model Exercise 1 as described in the *Modeling the Math*. Explain that since there are not enough ones to subtract, you must regroup 1 ten as 10 ones. Record each step. **Why are the 4 hundreds crossed out?** 1 hundred was regrouped as 10 tens.

Guided Practice Have students solve Exercise 2. Check students' answers. **How do you know when to regroup?** Regroup when there are not enough to subtract.

Independent Practice Assign Exercises 3–16. Note that Exercises 3 and 11 do not require regrouping. Exercises 2, 4, 7–9, 13, and 15 require only one regrouping.

● You may wish to also teach p. A9 before students work independently.

GO ON

Book A T13

2 Teach and Practice continued

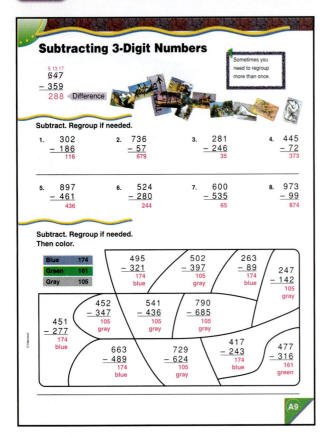

Teach Page A9 Have students use base-ten blocks to model the example problem. Show 6 hundreds, 4 tens, and 7 ones. Explain that you begin by subtracting the ones. **How can you subtract 9 ones from 7 ones?** Regroup 1 ten as 10 ones and subtract 9 ones from 17 ones. Continue to subtract from right to left.

Guided Practice Have students complete Exercise 1. Check students' answers. **How did you regroup 1 ten as 10 ones when there were no tens to regroup?** First, I regrouped 1 hundred as 10 tens and then I regrouped 1 ten as 10 ones.

Independent Practice Assign Exercises 2–8 and the puzzle.

- After students complete p. A9, continue instruction to teach p. A10.

Teach Page A10 Have students use base-ten blocks to model Exercise 1. Show 5 hundreds and 8 ones. Subtract the ones. Since there aren't enough tens to subtract, regroup 1 hundred as 10 tens and then subtract the tens. **How do you record regrouping in this exercise when using paper and pencil?** Cross out the digit 5 in the hundreds place and the digit 0 in the tens place. Write a small 4 above the hundreds place and a small 10 above the tens place.

Guided Practice Have students complete Exercise 2. Check students' answers. **How many times did you need to regroup before you were able to begin subtracting?** 2 times

Independent Practice Assign Exercises 3–20.

- After students complete p. A10, continue instruction to teach p. A11.

T14 First-Place Math

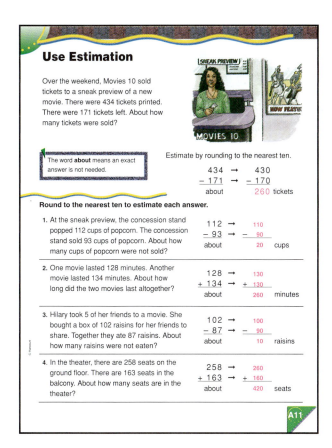

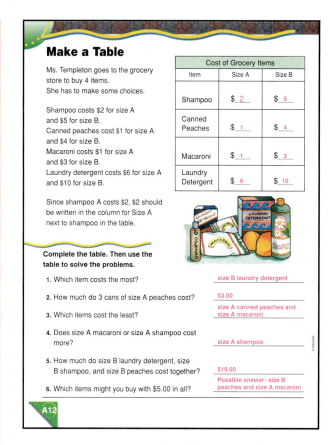

Teach Page A11 Draw 2 number lines on the chalkboard, the first one showing 430 to 440, and the second one showing 170 to 180. Explain how to round each number in the example problem to the nearest ten before finding the difference. **Why do you use estimation to solve this problem?** Since the question asks *about* how many tickets were sold, an exact answer is not required.

Guided Practice Have students solve Problem 1. Check students' answers. **Why should you round to the nearest ten instead of the nearest hundred?** Possible answer: Rounding to the nearest ten gives you an estimate that is closer to the exact difference.

Independent Practice Assign Problems 2–4. Note that Problems 2 and 4 involve addition and Problem 3 involves subtraction.

• After students complete p. A11, continue instruction to teach p. A12.

Teach Page A12 Define the vocabulary word for p. A12. Show students how to complete the table entries for the shampoo and the canned peaches. **Does size B shampoo cost more or less than size B canned peaches? Explain.** More; size B shampoo costs $5, and size B canned peaches costs $4, so the shampoo costs more.

Guided Practice Have students complete the table. Then have students solve Problem 1. Check students' work. **How do you know that laundry detergent costs the most?** When comparing the prices of all of the items, the size B laundry detergent has the greatest price.

Independent Practice Assign Problems 2–6.

3 Extra Practice

After students complete p. A12, you may wish to assign **Practice Activities**, p. P3.

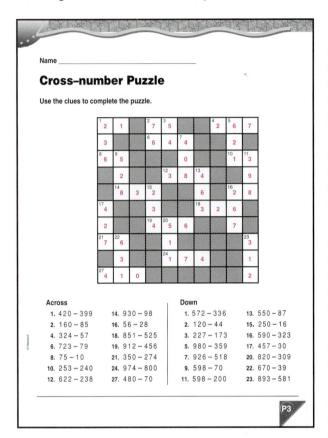

Teaching Notes

Teaching Notes

Week 1

Addition and Subtraction

DAY 4 At a Glance

Objectives

- To subtract 4-digit numbers

Problem Solving

- To make a graph to solve problems
- To find a pattern

1 Warm-Up Resources

- Number of the Day
- Problem of the Day
- Quick Review

page 4

2 Teach and Practice

Book A • Addition and Subtraction, pp. A13–A16

3 Extra Practice

Practice Activities, p. P4

---

1 Warm-Up Resources

Have students work the following problems. Discuss their strategies and solutions.

Number of the Day

Use the year you were born and the year of another person's birth. Find the sum of these two numbers. **Answers will vary.**

Problem of the Day

Draw pictures for steps 4 and 5.

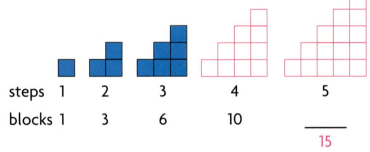

steps	1	2	3	4	5
blocks	1	3	6	10	15

Quick Review

1. Subtract: 718 − 355 **363**
2. Subtract: 400 − 287 **113**
3. Write the numbers from 0 to 35 counting by fives. **0, 5, 10, 15, 20, 25, 30, 35**
4. Given the pattern 7, 8, 9, 7, 8, 9, . . . , write a similar pattern using the digits 2, 3, and 4. **2, 3, 4, 2, 3, 4, . . .**

Vocabulary

| **bar graph** | a way to show information that uses bars to stand for data (p. A15) |
| **pattern** | a set of numbers or figures that have a relationship (p. A16) |

First-Place Math

2 Teach and Practice

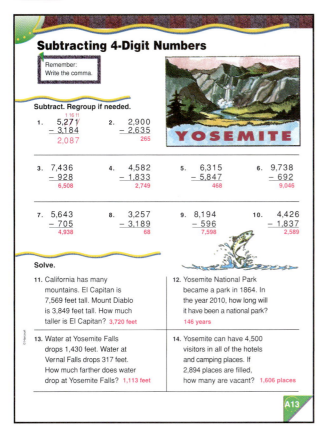

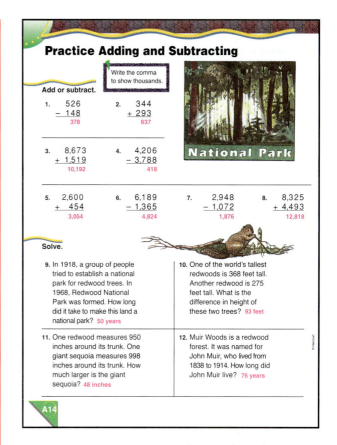

Teach Page A13 Direct students to look at Exercise 1. Remind students that when subtracting, they should always begin with the ones. Explain how regrouping is recorded in each place-value. **Why don't you need to regroup thousands?** There are enough thousands to subtract, so regrouping is not necessary. Complete Exercise 2 as a group. **How can you regroup 1 ten as 10 ones when there 0 tens?** First regroup 1 hundred as 10 tens, and then regroup 1 ten as 10 ones.

Guided Practice Have students solve Exercise 3. Check students' answers. **How many times did you regroup?** 2 times

Independent Practice Assign Exercises 4–14.

- After students complete p. A13, continue instruction to teach p. A14.

Teach Page A14 Use a place-value chart or grid paper to record Exercise 1. Review how to record regrouping. **How do you know if you need to regroup ones?** If there aren't enough ones to subtract, you need to regroup 1 ten as 10 ones before you can subtract.

Guided Practice Have students solve Exercise 2. Check students' answers. **How can you use estimation to check if your answer is reasonable?** Possible answer: Round each addend to the nearest hundred. 300 + 300 = 600; Since 637 is close to 600, the answer is reasonable.

Independent Practice Assign Exercises 3–12.

- After students complete p. A14, continue instruction to teach p. A15.

Book A T19

2 Teach and Practice continued

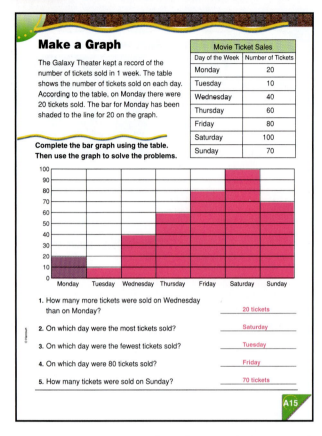

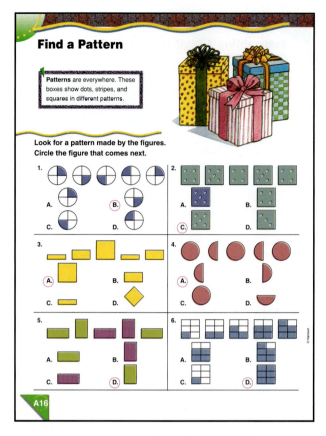

Teach Page A15 Define the vocabulary word for p. A15. Use the data from the table to shade in the bar for Tuesday's ticket sales. **What do the numbers on the left side of the bar graph represent?** number of tickets sold **What does each bar on the graph represent?** the number of tickets sold on that day

Guided Practice Have students complete the bar graph. Check students' graphs. **Why is it helpful to use an interval of 10 instead of an interval of 1 for this bar graph?** Possible answer: Since the number of tickets sold reached 100 on Saturday, using an interval of 10 keeps the graph from becoming too large. Ask students to solve Problem 1. Check students' answers.

Independent Practice Assign Problems 2–5.

- After students complete p. A15, continue instruction to teach p. A16.

Teach Page A16 Define the vocabulary word for p. A16. Draw a picture to model Problem 1. Number each part of the circle to help students identify which sections are shaded in each circle. **How can you describe the pattern?** Possible answer: The $\frac{1}{4}$ section of the circle that is shaded moves around the circle clockwise.

Guided Practice Have students solve Problem 2. Check students' answers. **If this pattern continues, how many dots will there be on the tenth figure in the pattern?** 5 dots

Independent Practice Assign Problems 3–6.

T20 First-Place Math

3 Extra Practice

After students complete p. A16, you may wish to assign **Practice Activities**, p. P4.

Teaching Notes

Book A T21

Week 1

Addition and Subtraction

DAY 5 At a Glance

Objectives
- To practice addition and subtraction
- To assess knowledge of addition, subtraction and problem solving

1 Warm-Up Resources
- Number of the Day
- Problem of the Day
- Quick Review

Daily Warm-Up Flip Chart, page 5

2 Teach and Practice
Book A • Addition and Subtraction, pp. A17–A18

3 Extra Practice
Practice Activities, pp. P5–P6
Game: Zoom

Manipulatives: Color tiles

4 Wrap Up and Assess
Addition and Subtraction Review, p. A19
Home Connection, p. A20
Book A Test, pp. 3–4

T22 First-Place Math

1 Warm-Up Resources

Have students work the following problems. Discuss their strategies and solutions.

Number of the Day
Add the year you were born to the current year.
Example: 1,993 + 2,002 = 3,995   Answers will vary.

Problem of the Day
There is a number that has twice as many thousands as ones, twice as many ones as hundreds, and twice as many hundreds as tens. What is the number?   Possible answer: 8,214

Quick Review
1. 507 − 324   183
2. 892 − 625   267
3. 3,212 + 4,508   7,720
4. 974 + 213   1,187

Vocabulary Review

Review vocabulary for Week 1.

addend	any of the numbers that are added (p. A1)
sum	the answer to an addition problem (p. A1)
regroup	to exchange amounts of equal value to rename a number (p. A1)
estimate	to find an answer that is close to the exact answer (p. A3)
round	to replace a number with another number that tells about how many (p. A3)
difference	the answer to a subtraction problem (p. A8)
table	a way to organize data using rows and columns (p. A12)
bar graph	a way to show information that uses bars to stand for data (p. A15)
pattern	a set of numbers or figures that have a relationship (p. A16)

2 Teach and Practice

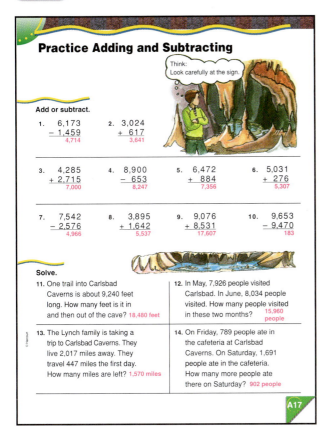

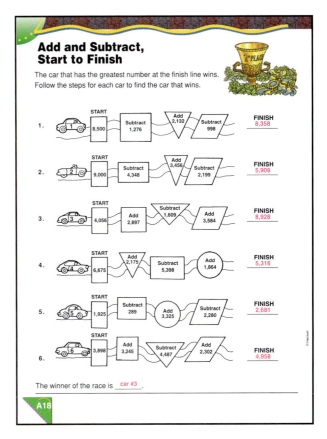

Teach Page A17 Direct students' attention to Exercise 1. **How do you know whether to add or subtract?** The minus sign is used, so you subtract. Solve Exercise 1 step-by-step with students. Explain how to record regrouping when necessary.

Guided Practice Have students solve Exercise 2. Check students' answers. **Did you need to regroup ones? Explain.** Yes; 7 ones + 4 ones = 11 ones, which is 1 ten 1 one.

Independent Practice Assign Exercises 3–14.

• You may wish to also teach p. A18 before students work independently.

Teach Page A18 Use grid paper to record the first part of Exercise 1. Grid paper is found on p. A21. Explain how to line up the place-value columns. **How many problems will you solve to find the Finish number for Car #1?** 3

Guided Practice Have students complete Exercise 1. Check students' answers. **What is another way to solve this problem?** Possible answer: Begin by adding 2,132 to 8,500 to get 10,632. Add 1,276 and 998 to find the total amount to subtract, 2,274. Then subtract 2,274 from 10,632.

Independent Practice Assign Exercises 2–6 and have students find the winner of the race.

3 Extra Practice

After students complete p. A18, you may wish to assign **Practice Activities**, pp. P5–P6.

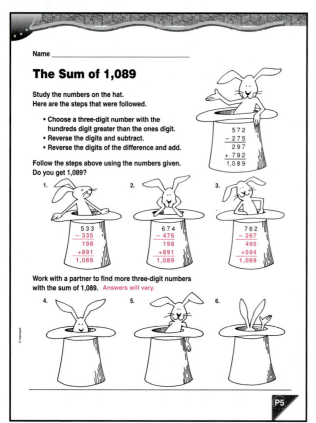

- You may also wish to have students play the game *Zoom* to practice addition and subtraction.

4 Wrap Up and Assess

Have students complete p. A19 to prepare for the Test.

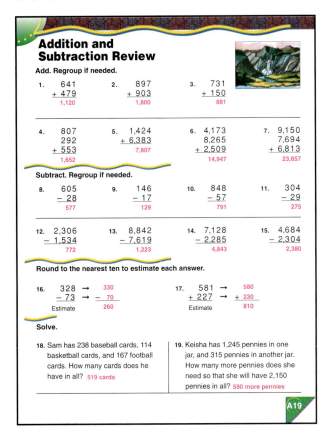

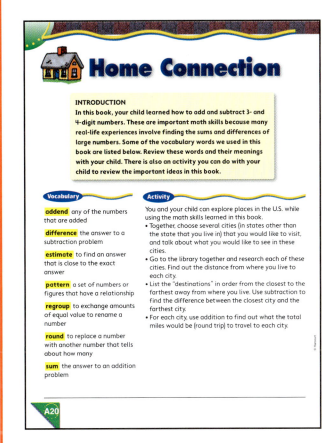

Use the following information to determine which pages students should review before taking the Test for Book A.

Review Items	Skill	Review
1–4	Add 3-Digit Numbers	A1–A2
5–7	Add 4-Digit Numbers	A4–A5
8	Subtract Across Zeros	A10
9–10	3-Digit Subtraction	A8–A9
11	Subtract Across Zeros	A10
12–15	Subtract 4-Digit Numbers	A13
16–17	Use Estimation	A11
18–19	Practice Adding and Subtracting	A14, A17, A18

Review the Home Connection page with students. You may want to preview the activity with students so they can explain it to their parents.

Test

Have students complete the Test (**Assessment**, pp. 3–4) for Book A • Addition and Subtraction.

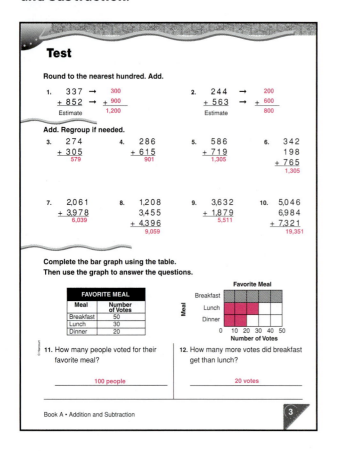
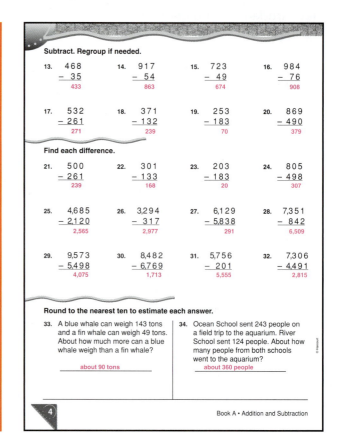

Test Items	Skill	Review
1–2	Estimate Sums to the Hundreds	A3
3–6	Add 3-Digit Numbers	A1–A2
7–10	Add 4-Digit Numbers	A4–A5
11–12	Make a Graph	A15
13–20	3-Digit Subtraction	A8–A9
21–24	Subtract Across Zeros	A10
25–32	Subtract 4-Digit Numbers	A13
33–34	Use Estimation	A11

Check What Students Know
If a student answers an item incorrectly, refer to the "Review" column to determine where the related skill is taught. You may wish to record students' results on their record forms. (**Assessment**, p. 25)

T26 First-Place Math

Teaching Notes

Week 2 Planner

OBJECTIVES
SKILLS
- To multiply 2-, 3-, and 4-digit numbers by 1-digit numbers
- To multiply 2- and 3-digit numbers by 2-digit numbers
- To divide 2- and 3-digit numbers by 1-digit divisors
- To check division
- To divide 2- and 3-digit numbers by 2-digit divisors

	DAY 1 pages T30–T35	**DAY 2** pages T36–T39
1 Warm-Up	**WARM-UP RESOURCES** Number of the Day, p. 6 Problem of the Day, p. 6 Quick Review, p. 6	**WARM-UP RESOURCES** Number of the Day, p. 7 Problem of the Day, p. 7 Quick Review, p. 7
2 Teach and Practice	Facts Practice, p. B1 Multiplying 2-Digit Numbers, p. B2 Multiplying 3-Digit Numbers, p. B3 Multiplying 4-Digit Numbers, p. B4	Multiplying 2-Digit Numbers, pp. B5–B6 Work Backwards, p. B7
3 Extra Practice	Alphabet Multiplication, p. P7	Practice Multiplying, p. P8
4 Wrap Up and Assess	**PRETEST** Book B Pretest, pp. 5–6 Assess knowledge of multiplication, division, and problem solving	

T28 First-Place Math

Multiplication and Division

OBJECTIVES (CONTINUED)
PROBLEM SOLVING
- To solve problems by working backwards
- To solve problems using multiple steps
- To solve problems by choosing the operation

DAY 3 pages T40–T43	DAY 4 pages T44–T49	DAY 5 pages T50–T55
WARM-UP RESOURCES Number of the Day, p. 8 Problem of the Day, p. 8 Quick Review, p. 8	**WARM-UP RESOURCES** Number of the Day, p. 9 Problem of the Day, p. 9 Quick Review, p. 9	**WARM-UP RESOURCES** Number of the Day, p. 10 Problem of the Day, p. 10 Quick Review, p. 10
Multiplying 3-Digit Numbers, pp. B8–B9 Multi-Step Problems, p. B10	Dividing 2-Digit Numbers, p. B11 Dividing 3-Digit Numbers, pp. B12–B13 Checking Division, p. B14 Choose the Operation, p. B15	Dividing by 2-Digit Divisors, pp. B16–B17 Practice Multiplying and Dividing, p. B18
Missing Multiplication Digits, p. P9	Using Remainder Clues, p. P10	Dividing by 2-Digit Divisors, p. P11 Facts Practice, p. P12 Game: *Zoom*
		WRAP UP Review, p. B19 Home Connection, p. B20 **TEST** Book B Test, pp. 7–8 Assess knowledge of multiplication, division, and problem solving

Book B T29

Week 2

Multiplication and Division

DAY 1 At a Glance

Objectives
- To assess knowledge of multiplication and division and problem solving
- To multiply 2-, 3-, and 4-digit numbers by 1-digit numbers

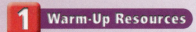
1 Warm-Up Resources
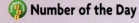 Number of the Day
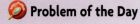 Problem of the Day
⏱ Quick Review

Book B Pretest, pp. 5–6

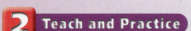
2 Teach and Practice

Book B • Multiplication and Division, pp. B1–B4

Manipulatives:
  Two-color counters
  Base-ten blocks

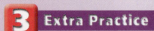
3 Extra Practice

Practice Activities, p. P7

T30 First-Place Math

---

1 Warm-Up Resources

Have students work the following problems. Discuss their strategies and solutions.

Number of the Day

Write four multiplication sentences with the number of hours in a day as the product. **Possible answers: $1 \times 24 = 24$; $24 \times 1 = 24$; $2 \times 12 = 24$; $12 \times 2 = 24$; $3 \times 8 = 24$; $8 \times 3 = 24$; $4 \times 6 = 24$; $6 \times 4 = 24$**

Problem of the Day

Emily paints letters on T-shirts. It takes her 10 minutes to paint each letter. She has 2 hours to work and wants to complete a T-shirt that says HAVE A NICE DAY. Will she be able to complete the T-shirt in that time? Explain. **Yes; it will take exactly 2 hours to complete the T-shirt. 10 min $\times$ 12 = 120 min = 2 hours**

Quick Review

1. $12 + 12 + 12 =$ **36**   2. $25 + 25 + 25 =$ **75**
3. $31 + 31 =$ **62**   4. $40 + 40 + 40 =$ **120**

Vocabulary

multiplication — the process of finding the total number of items made up of equal-size groups or of finding the total number of items in a given number of groups (p. B1)

division — the process of sharing a number of items to find how many groups can be made or how many items will be in a group (p. B1)

factor — a number that is multiplied by another number to find a product (p. B3)

Pretest

Have students complete the Pretest (Assessment, pp. 5–6) for Book B • Multiplication and Division.

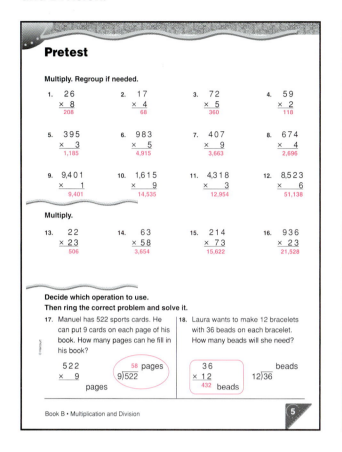
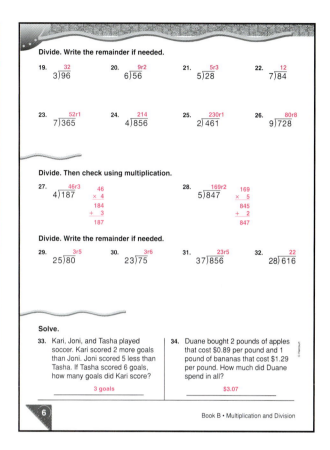

Pretest Items	Skill	Review
1–4	Multiply 2-Digit Numbers	B2
5–8	Multiply 3-Digit Numbers	B3
9–12	Multiply 4-Digit Numbers	B4
13–14	Multiply 2-Digit Numbers (by 2-Digit Numbers)	B5–B6
15–16	Multiply 3-Digit Numbers (by 2-Digit Numbers)	B8–B9
17–18	Choose the Operation	B15
19–22	Divide 2-Digit Numbers	B11
23–26	Divide 3-Digit Numbers	B12–B13
27–28	Checking Division	B14
29–32	Divide by 2-Digit Divisors	B16–B17
33	Work Backwards	B7
34	Multi-Step Problems	B10

Check What Students Know

If a student answers an item incorrectly, refer to the "Review" column to determine where the related skill is taught. You may wish to record students' results on their record forms. (**Assessment**, p. 26)

2 Teach and Practice

For an introductory activity using counters, see *More Manipulative Activities*, p. T177.

Modeling the Math

Use counters to model 4 × 5. Then have students use counters to work similar problems.

1. Show 4 groups.

2. Place 5 counters in each group. Add to find the product.

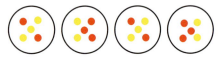

5 + 5 + 5 + 5 = 20

So, 4 × 5 = 20.

Have students use counters to model 32 ÷ 4.

1. Use 32 counters. Show 4 groups.

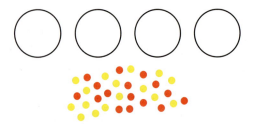

2. Place a counter in each group.

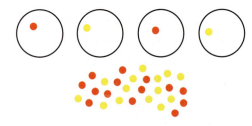

3. Continue until all counters are used.

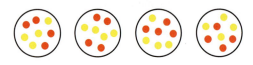

So, 32 ÷ 4 = 8.

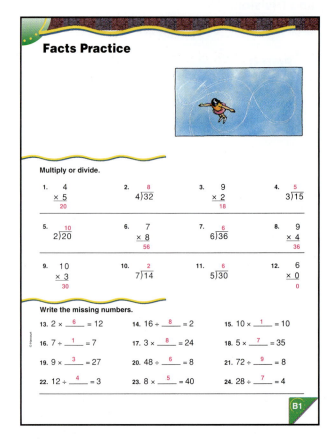

Teach Page B1 Define the vocabulary words for p. B1. Use counters to model Exercises 1 and 2, as described in the *Modeling the Math*. **What does it mean to multiply?** to combine equal groups; **to divide?** to separate into equal groups Use counters to model Exercise 13. Separate 12 counters into 2 equal groups of 6. **How is solving Exercise 13 like solving a division problem?** Possible answer: You can think of separating 12 into 2 equal groups to find the missing number.

Guided Practice Have students solve Exercise 14. Check students' answers. **What multiplication sentence can you think of to find the missing number?** 2 × 8 = 16

Independent Practice Assign Exercises 3–12 and 15–24.

• After students complete p. B1, continue instruction to teach p. B2.

First-Place Math

For an introductory activity using base-ten blocks, see *More Manipulative Activities*, p. T176.

Modeling the Math

Use base-ten blocks to model 38 × 7. Then have students use base-ten blocks to work similar problems.

1. Model 7 groups of 38.
   Multiply the ones.

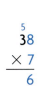

$$\begin{array}{r} \overset{5}{3}8 \\ \times\ 7 \\ \hline 6 \end{array}$$

7 × 8 ones = 56 ones
Regroup 56 ones as 5 tens 6 ones.

2. Multiply the tens.

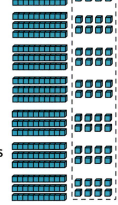

$$\begin{array}{r} \overset{5}{3}8 \\ \times\ 7 \\ \hline 266 \end{array}$$

7 × 3 tens = 21 tens
Add the regrouped 5 tens.

5 tens + 21 tens = 26 tens, or 2 hundreds 6 tens.

So, 38 × 7 = 266.

Teach Page B2 Use base-ten blocks to model Exercise 1, as described in the *Modeling the Math*. When modeling the exercise, show how to record regrouped numbers. **How many ones are regrouped as tens?** 50 ones are regrouped as 5 tens.

Guided Practice Have students solve Exercise 2. Check students' answers. **How did you record regrouping 10 ones as 1 ten?** by writing a small one above the tens column

Independent Practice Assign Exercises 3–22.

● You may wish to also teach p. B3 before students work independently.

2 Teach and Practice continued

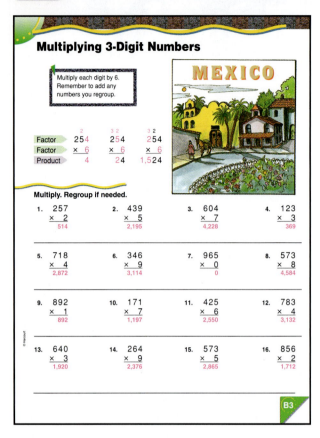

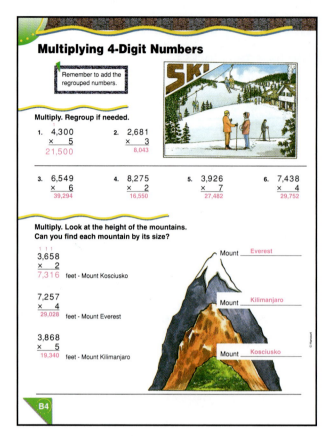

Teach Page B3 Define the vocabulary word for p. B3. Use base-ten blocks to model the example exercise. Multiply the ones. Explain how to record the regrouped numbers. When multiplying the tens, ask, **What should be done with the 2 regrouped tens?** Add them to the product of the tens. Show how to record regrouping and then multiply the hundreds.

Guided Practice Have students solve Exercise 1. Check students' answers. **How many times did you regroup?** 2 times

Independent Practice Assign Exercises 2–16. Note that Exercises 4, 7, and 9 do not require regrouping.

• You may wish to also teach p. B4 before students work independently.

Teach Page B4 Explain how to solve Exercise 1 by multiplying in each place-value position starting with the ones. **Why is there a small 1 above the thousands place?** 5 × 3 hundreds = 15 hundreds, which is 1 thousand 5 hundreds. The regrouped thousand is recorded above the thousands place.

Guided Practice Have students solve Exercise 2. Check students' answers. **What are the steps used to multiply 4-digit numbers?** Possible answer: Multiply the ones, the tens, the hundreds, and the thousands, and add any regrouped numbers.

Independent Practice Assign Exercises 3–6. Next, have students multiply to find the height of each mountain and then label the mountains.

T34 First-Place Math

3 Extra Practice

After students complete p. B4, you may wish to assign **Practice Activities**, p. P7.

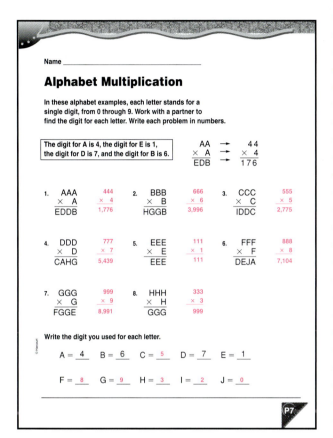

Book B T35

Week 2

Multiplication and Division

DAY 2 At a Glance

Objectives
- To multiply by 2-digit numbers

Problem Solving
- To solve problems by working backwards

1 Warm-Up Resources
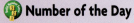 Number of the Day
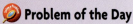 Problem of the Day
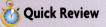 Quick Review

2 Teach and Practice

Book B • Multiplication and Division, pp. B5–B7

Manipulatives:
　Two-color counters
　Base-ten blocks

3 Extra Practice

Practice Activities, p. P8

T36 First-Place Math

---

1 Warm-Up Resources

Have students work the following problems. Discuss their strategies and solutions.

Number of the Day
The number of the day is a two-digit number in which the digit in the ones place is three more than the digit in the tens place. Also, the digit in the ones place is twice as many as the digit in the tens place. What is the number? **36**

Problem of the Day
Kyle runs 8 miles. He runs the first 2 miles in 14 minutes. He runs the next 2 miles in 18 minutes and the 2 miles after that in 22 minutes. If he continues this pattern, how long will it take him to run all 8 miles? **80 minutes or 1 hour 20 minutes**

Quick Review
1. $9 \times 40 =$ **360**　　2. $5 \times 50 =$ **250**
3. $10 \times 30 =$ **300**　　4. $12 \times 40 =$ **480**

Vocabulary
product — the answer to a multiplication problem (p. B5)

2 Teach and Practice

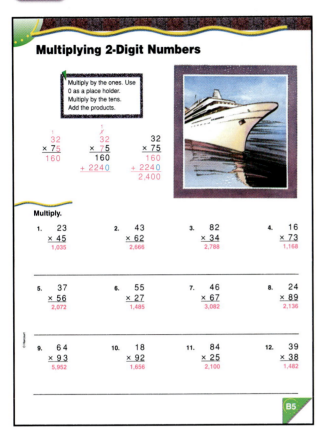

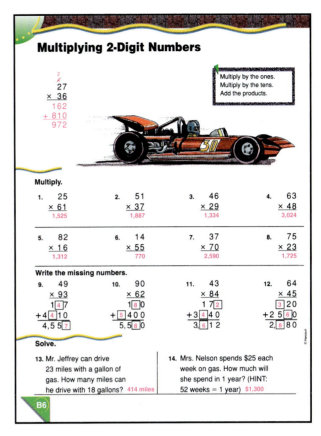

Teach Page B5 Define the vocabulary word for p. B5. Write 32 × 75 vertically on the board. Talk through each step to find partial products, as shown here.

```
    32
   ×75
    10  (5 × 2)
   150  (5 × 30)
   140  (70 × 2)
 +2,100 (70 × 30)
  2,400
```

Next, explain the steps for solving the example exercise shown on the student page. Have students use grid paper, on page B21, to help them record digits in the correct place-value columns. **When you compare the partial products in both problems, what do you notice?** The sum of the partial products 10 and 150 is the same as the 160 in the example exercise.

Guided Practice Have students solve Exercise 1. **Which method did you use? Why?** Answers will vary.

Independent Practice Assign Exercises 2–12.

- You may wish to also teach p. B6 before students work independently.

Teach Page B6 Direct students to look at the example exercise. Talk through each step of the multiplication, pointing out the use of the zero as a place holder. **Why are the 4 regrouped tens crossed out?** so that they are not added when multiplying tens

Guided Practice Have students solve Exercise 1. Check students' answers. **What is the product of the ones?** 25 **the tens?** 1,500

Independent Practice Assign Exercises 2–14.

- After students complete p. B6, continue instruction to teach p. B7.

GO ON

Book B T37

3 Extra Practice

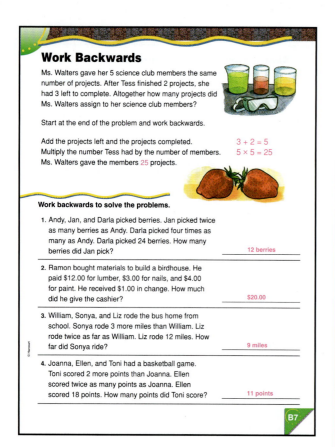

After students complete p. B7, you may wish to assign **Practice Activities,** p. P8.

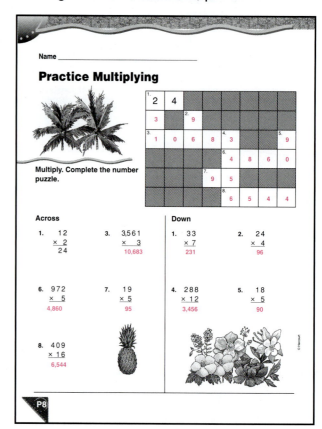

Teach Page B7 Draw a picture to model the example problem. Use circles to show 5 club members. In each circle, write 5 to represent Tess's projects. Then, to represent 5 projects for each of the 5 club members. The total number of projects is 25.

were used to solve the problem: addition and multiplication.

Guided Practice
Problem 1. Check students' work on the problem. The answer is 6 berries.

Independent Practice

Teaching Notes

Week 2
Multiplication and Division

DAY 3 At a Glance

Objectives
- To multiply 3-digit numbers by 2-digit numbers

Problem Solving
- To solve problems using multiple steps

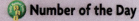 **Warm-Up Resources**
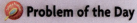 Number of the Day
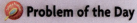 Problem of the Day
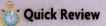 Quick Review

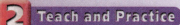 **Teach and Practice**

Book B • Multiplication and Division, pp. B8–B10

Manipulatives:
Play money

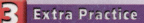 **Extra Practice**

Practice Activities, p. P9

---

1 Warm-Up Resources

Have students work the following problems. Discuss their strategies and solutions.

Number of the Day
Calculate the number of minutes it takes for you to walk from class to the playground. Multiply this number by 10 to find how much time you would spend going to and from the playground in 5 round trips. **Possible answer: 5 × 10 = 50 minutes**

Problem of the Day
Bill, Mark, Jenny, and April are playing a video game. Jenny's score is three times Mark's score but 5 points less than April's score. April's score is twice Bill's score. Mark's score is 65. What is each friend's score? **Mark: 65; Bill: 100; Jenny: 195; April: 200.**

Quick Review
1. 3 × 123 = **369**
2. 60 × 500 = **30,000**
3. 45 × 800 = **36,000**
4. 12 × 200 = **2,400**

Vocabulary

multiplication   the process of finding the total number of items made up of equal-size groups or of finding the total number of items in a given number of groups **(p. B8)**

T40 First-Place Math

2 Teach and Practice

Multiplying 3-Digit Numbers

Multiply by the ones. Use 0 as a place holder. Then multiply by the tens. Add the products.

```
  1 1         2 3
  568         568         568
 × 42        × 42        × 42
 1136        1136        1136
           + 22720     + 22720
                        23,856
```

Multiply.

1. 271 × 61 = 16,531
2. 627 × 38 = 23,826
3. 900 × 64 = 57,600
4. 586 × 23 = 13,478
5. 754 × 70 = 52,780
6. 382 × 55 = 21,010
7. 839 × 98 = 82,222
8. 165 × 82 = 13,530
9. 470 × 23 = 10,810
10. 698 × 79 = 55,142
11. 553 × 16 = 8,848
12. 346 × 67 = 23,182

B8

Multiplying 3-Digit Numbers

```
  471
 × 23
10,833
```

Multiply.

1. 125 × 63 = 7,875
2. 743 × 82 = 60,926
3. 608 × 47 = 28,576
4. 376 × 19 = 7,144
5. 867 × 31 = 26,877
6. 222 × 56 = 12,432
7. 531 × 74 = 39,294
8. 914 × 90 = 82,260
9. 459 × 15 = 6,885
10. 982 × 68 = 66,776
11. 326 × 32 = 10,432
12. 791 × 75 = 59,325
13. 615 × 51 = 31,365
14. 242 × 24 = 5,808
15. 500 × 40 = 20,000
16. 837 × 36 = 30,132
17. 394 × 87 = 34,278
18. 763 × 19 = 14,497
19. 188 × 92 = 17,296
20. 454 × 46 = 20,884

B9

Teach Page B8 Define the vocabulary word for p. B8. Solve the example exercise. First, multiply by the ones and then by the tens. Next, add the products. **How can you use estimation to check whether the answer is reasonable?** Possible answer: 40 × 600 = 24,000; since 23,856 is close to 24,000, the answer is reasonable.

Guided Practice Have students solve Exercise 1. Check students' answers. **When did you need to regroup?** when multiplying tens; 7 tens × 6 tens = 42 tens, or 4 hundreds 2 tens.

Independent Practice Assign Exercises 2–12.

- You may wish to also teach p. B9 before students work independently.

Teach Page B9 Solve the example exercise. First, multiply by the ones and then by the tens. Then add the products. When multiplying by the tens, ask, **What is the ones digit in the prod**

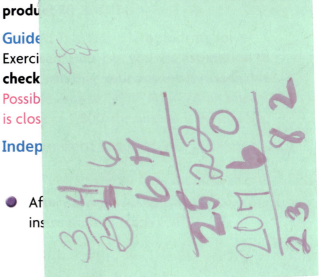

Book B T41

3 Extra Practice

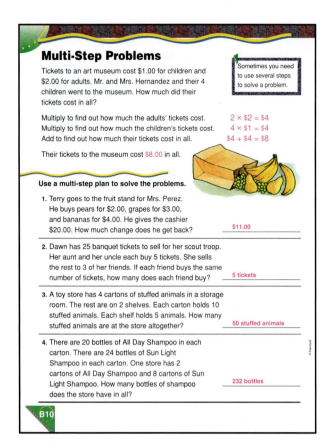

After students complete p. B10, you may wish to assign **Practice Activities**, p. P9.

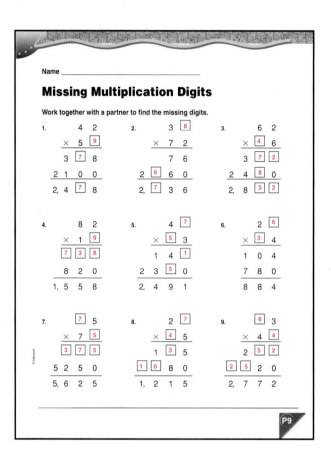

Teach Page B10 Use play money to model the example problem. Show 2 groups of $2 for the adult tickets and four $1 bills for the children's tickets. **How can this problem be solved using only addition?** Add the cost of each of the tickets; $2 + $2 + $1 + $1 + $1 + $1 = $8.

Guided Practice Have students solve Problem 1. Check students' work. **What are two different ways you can solve this problem?** Add the cost of all the fruit and subtract the total cost from the amount paid to find the change; subtract the cost of each type of fruit from the amount paid, one at a time.

Independent Practice Assign Problems 2–4.

T42 First-Place Math

Teaching Notes

Week 2

Multiplication and Division

DAY 4 At a Glance

Objectives

- To divide 2- and 3-digit numbers by 1-digit numbers
- To check division

Problem Solving

- To solve problems by choosing the operation

1 Warm-Up Resources

- Number of the Day
- Problem of the Day
- Quick Review

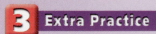

2 Teach and Practice

Book B • Multiplication and Division, pp. B11–B15

Manipulatives: Base-ten blocks

3 Extra Practice

Practice Activities, p. P10

T44 First-Place Math

1 Warm-Up Resources

Have students work the following problems. Discuss their strategies and solutions.

Number of the Day

Write a fact family for multiplication and division that includes the number 12. **Possible answer:**
$12 \times 2 = 24$; $2 \times 12 = 24$; $24 \div 12 = 2$; $24 \div 2 = 12$

Problem of the Day

Steve and Donna each hit the target with three darts, and they both got the same score. Steve never hit the 1, nor did he hit the same number every time. What was each one's score? **11 or 13**
How did he or she get it? **Possible answer: Either Steve hit 5, 3, 3, and Donna hit 5, 5, 1 or they both hit 5, 5, 3 or 5, 3, 3.**

Quick Review

1. $15 \div 5 =$ **3**
2. $48 \div 4 =$ **12**
3. $160 \div 8 =$ **20**
4. $270 \div 9 =$ **30**

Vocabulary

quotient	the answer, not including the remainder, in a division problem (p. B11)
dividend	the number that is to be divided in a division problem (p. B11)
divisor	the number that divides the dividend (p. B11)
remainder	the amount left over after you find a quotient (p. B11)

2 Teach and Practice

For an introductory activity using base-ten blocks, see *More Manipulative Activities*, p. T176.

Modeling the Math

Use base-ten blocks to model 79 ÷ 3. Then have students use base-ten blocks to work similar problems.

1. Show 79 as 7 tens 9 ones. Draw circles to show 3 equal groups.

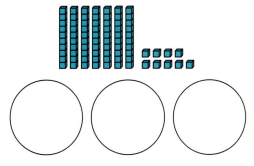

2. Divide the tens first. Place an equal number of tens into each group.

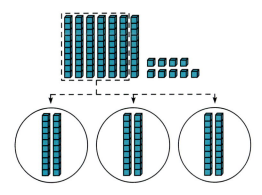

3. Regroup 1 ten 9 ones as 19 ones. Place an equal number of ones into each group. Record the quotient and the remainder.

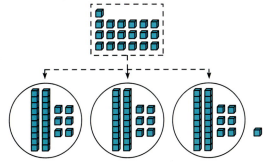

So, 79 ÷ 3 = 26 r1.

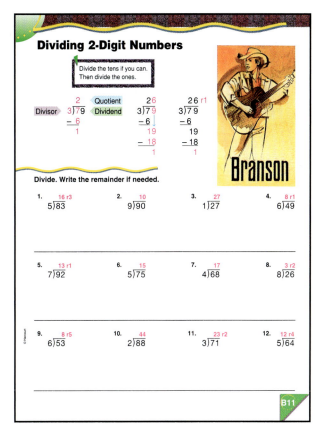

Teach Page B11 Define the vocabulary words for p. B11. Use base-ten blocks to model 7 tens and 9 ones being divided into 3 equal groups, as described in the *Modeling the Math*. Divide the tens. Regroup the extra ten as 10 ones. Divide the ones. Record the remainder. **How was regrouping the extra ten recorded in the example exercise?** The 9 ones were brought down so that 19 ones were being divided by 3.

Guided Practice Have students solve Exercises 1 and 4. Check students' answers. **In Exercise 4 how do you know the quotient will be a 1-digit number?** Since $6 \times 10 = 60$ and $49 < 60$, the quotient will be less than 10, or a 1-digit number.

Independent Practice Assign Exercises 2–3 and 5–12.

• After students complete p. B11, continue instruction to teach p. B12.

2 Teach and Practice continued

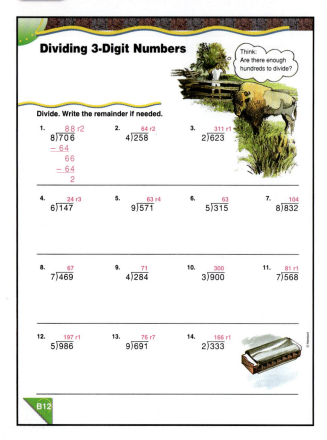

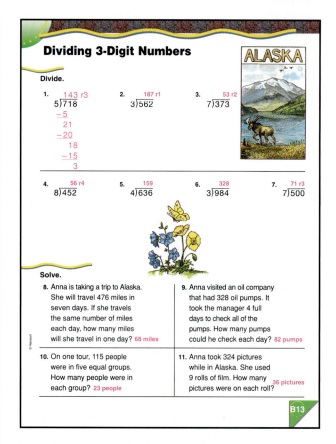

Teach Page B12 Use base-ten blocks to model 7 hundreds 6 ones divided into 8 equal groups. Regroup the hundreds as tens and divide the tens. Regroup the extra tens as ones and divide all of the ones. Record the remainder. **Why are the hundreds regrouped as tens before beginning to divide?** There are not enough hundreds to divide into 8 groups.

Guided Practice Have students solve Exercise 2. Check students' answers. **How can you use estimation to decide where to place the first digit in the quotient?** Since $240 \div 4 = 60$, the first digit in the quotient will be in the tens place.

Independent Practice Assign Exercises 3–14. Note that Exercises 6–10 do not have remainders.

- You may wish to also teach p. B13 before students work independently.

Teach Page B13 Show students the steps to solve Exercise 1. Explain how to divide, multiply, subtract, and compare in each step. **What basic division facts were used to solve this exercise?** $5 \div 5 = 1$; $20 \div 5 = 4$; $15 \div 5 = 3$

Guided Practice Direct students' attention to Exercise 3. **How do you know where to place the first digit in the quotient?** Possible answer: Since you can't divide 3 into 7 equal groups, think of regrouping the hundreds as tens and divide 37 tens by 7. Have students find the quotient and remainder. Check students' answers.

Independent Practice Assign Exercises 2 and 4–11.

- After students complete p. B13, continue instruction to teach p. B14.

T46 First-Place Math

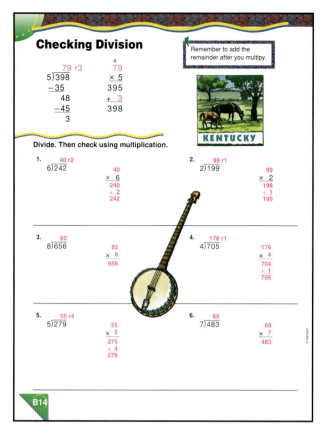

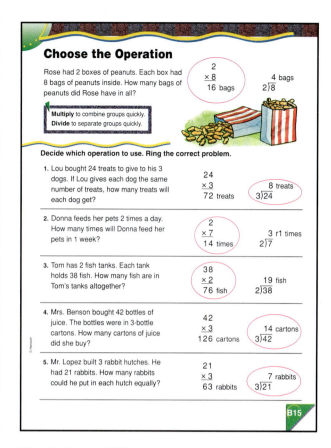

Teach Page B14 Show students how to find the quotient in the example exercise. **What does the answer, 79 r3, mean?** It means that when you try to divide 398 into 5 equal groups, you will have 79 in each of the groups, and there will be 3 left over. Explain that multiplication can be used to check division by combining equal groups and then adding the remainder to the product to get the dividend.

Guided Practice Have students solve Exercise 1. Check students' answers. **How do you know when you are finished dividing?** When you have divided in each place-value and the remainder is less than the divisor.

Independent Practice Assign Exercises 2–6.

● After students complete p. B14, continue instruction to teach p. B15.

Teach Page B15 Direct students' attention to the example problem. **How do you know which operation to use to solve this problem?** Since equal groups are being combined, 8 bags in each of 2 boxes, multiplication is used.

Guided Practice Have students solve Problem 1. Check students' work. **How can this problem be solved using a different operation?** Subtraction could be used to take away groups of 3 from 24.

Independent Practice Assign Problems 2–5.

Book B

3 Extra Practice

After students complete p. B15, you may wish to assign **Practice Activities,** p. P10.

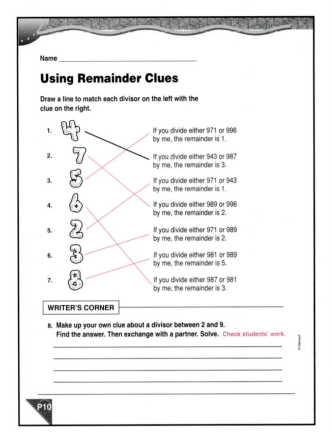

Teaching Notes

T48 First-Place Math

Teaching Notes

Week 2

Multiplication and Division

DAY 5 At a Glance

Objectives
- To divide by 2-digit numbers
- To assess knowledge of multiplication, division, and problem solving

- Number of the Day
- Problem of the Day
- Quick Review

page 10

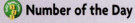

Book B • Multiplication and Division, pp. B16–B18

Manipulatives: Base-ten blocks

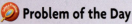

Practice Activities, pp. P11–P12
Game: Zoom

Manipulatives: Color tiles

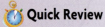

Multiplication and Division Review, p. B19
Home Connection, p. B20
Book B Test, Assessment, pp. 7–8

T50 First-Place Math

1 Warm-Up Resources

Have students work the following problems. Discuss their strategies and solutions.

Number of the Day
Find the number that is a multiple of 10 and is the divisor in a problem that has a quotient of 5 and a dividend less than 150. What is that number? **10 or 20**

Problem of the Day
Choose a 2-digit or 3-digit number. Multiply it by 6. Add 14. Divide by 2. Subtract 4. Divide by 3. Subtract the number that you started with from this number. What do you notice? **The answer is always 1, no matter what number you choose.**

Quick Review
1. 210 ÷ 30 = **7**
2. 80 ÷ 7 = **11r3**
3. 134 ÷ 4 = **33r2**
4. 400 ÷ 80 = **5**

Vocabulary

Review the vocabulary for Week 2.

factor	a number that is multiplied by another number to find a product (p. B3)
product	the answer to a multiplication problem (p. B5)
dividend	the number that is to be divided in a division problem (p. B11)
divisor	the number that divides the dividend (p. B11)
quotient	the answer, not including the remainder, in a division problem (p. B11)
remainder	the amount left over after you find a quotient (p. B11)

2 Teach and Practice

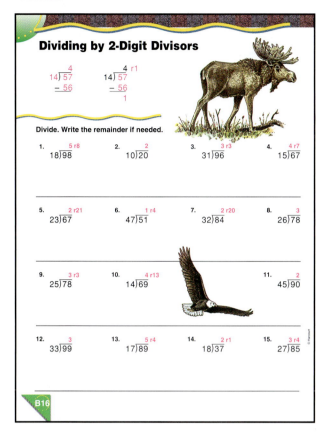

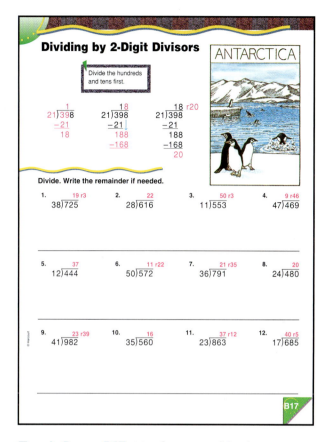

Teach Page B16 Use base-ten blocks to model the example exercise. Show 5 tens and 7 ones. Then regroup 1 ten and separate the blocks into groups of 14. **How many groups of 14 are in 57?** 4 **Are there any left over?** Yes; 1 is left over.

Guided Practice Have students solve Exercise 1. **How can you use multiplication to check your answer?** 5 × 18 = 90, 90 + 8 = 98; since 98 is the dividend, the answer is correct.

Independent Practice Assign Exercises 2–15. Note that Exercises 2, 8, 11, and 12 do not have remainders.

- You may wish to also teach p. B17 before students work independently.

Teach Page B17 Use base-ten blocks to model the example exercise. Show 3 hundreds 9 tens 8 ones divided into groups of 21. Explain how each step is recorded. **How can you use multiplication to check your answer?** 18 × 21 = 378, 378 + 20 = 398; since the dividend is 398, the answer is correct.

Guided Practice Have students solve Exercise 1. Check students' answers. **Would there be a remainder if the problem were changed to 722 ÷ 38?** no

Independent Practice Assign Exercises 2–12. Note that Exercises 2, 5, 8, and 10 do not have remainders.

- After students complete p. B17, continue instruction to teach p. B18.

Book B T51

2 Teach and Practice continued

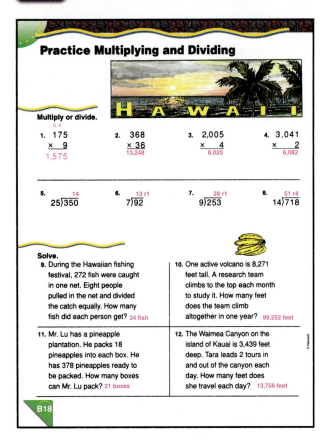

Teach Page B18 Show students how to solve Exercises 1 and 5. Review how to record regrouping when multiplying and how to record the steps in the division process. **How can you check your answer for Exercise 5?** Multiply; 14 × 25 = 350; since the dividend is 350, the answer is correct.

Guided Practice Have students solve Exercises 2 and 3. Check students' answers. **How can you use estimation to check whether your answer to Exercise 3 is reasonable?** Possible answer: 2,000 × 4 = 8,000; since 8,020 is close to 8,000, the answer is reasonable.

Independent Practice Assign Exercises 4 and 6–12.

Teaching Notes

3 Extra Practice

After students complete p. B18, you may wish to assign **Practice Activities**, pp. P11–P12.

- You may also wish to have students play the game *Zoom* to practice multiplication and division.

4 Wrap Up and Assess

Have students complete p. B19 to prepare for the Test.

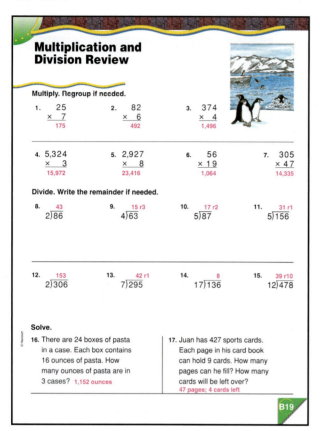

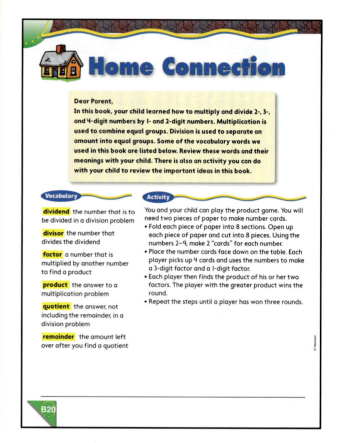

Review the Home Connection page with students. You may want to preview the activity with students so they can explain it to their parents.

Use the following information to determine which pages students should review before taking the Book B Test.

Review Items	Skill	Review
1–5	Multiply 2-, 3-, and 4-Digit Numbers	B2, B3, B4
6–7	Multiply 2- and 3-Digit Numbers (by 2-Digit Numbers)	B5–B6, B8–B9
8–10	Divide 2-Digit Numbers	B11
11–13	Divide 3-Digit Numbers	B12–B13
14–15	Divide by 2-Digit Divisors	B16–B17
16–17	Practice Multiplying and Dividing	B18

T54 First-Place Math

Test

Have students complete the Test (Assessment, pp. 7-8) for Book B • Multiplication and Division.

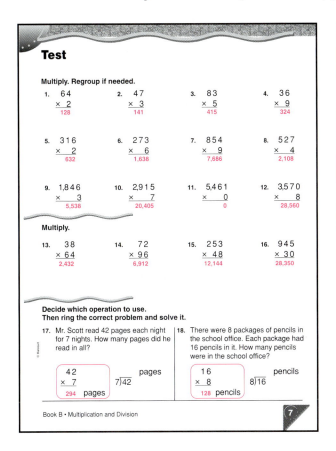
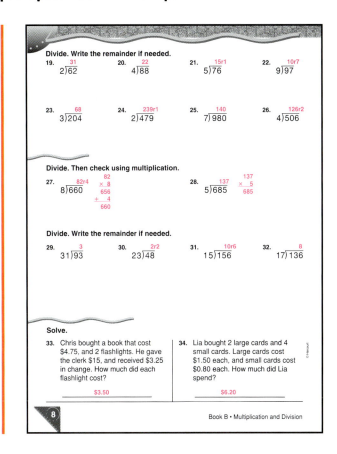

Test Items	Skill	Review
1–4	Multiply 2-Digit Numbers	B2
5–8	Multiply 3-Digit Numbers	B3
9–12	Multiply 4-Digit Numbers	B4
13–14	Multiply 2-Digit Numbers (by 2-Digit Numbers)	B5–B6
15–16	Multiply 3-Digit Numbers (by 2-Digit Numbers)	B8–B9
17–18	Choose the Operation	B15
19–22	Divide 2-Digit Numbers	B11
23–26	Divide 3-Digit Numbers	B12–B13
27–28	Check Division	B14
29–32	Divide by 2-Digit Divisors	B16–B17
33	Work Backwards	B7
34	Multi-Step Problems	B10

Check What Students Know

If a student answers an item incorrectly, refer to the "Review" column to determine where the related skill is taught. You may wish to record students' results on their record forms. (Assessment, p. 26)

Week 3 Planner

OBJECTIVES

SKILLS

- To find equivalent fractions
- To write fractions in simplest form
- To understand and write mixed numbers
- To add and subtract like fractions and express answers in simplest form
- To add and subtract mixed numbers
- To add and subtract like mixed numbers and record the answer in simplest form
- To add and subtract unlike fractions using models

	DAY 1 pages T58–T63	**DAY 2** pages T64–T69
1 Warm-Up	**WARM-UP RESOURCES** Number of the Day, p. 11 Problem of the Day, p. 11 Quick Review, p. 11	**WARM-UP RESOURCES** Number of the Day, p. 12 Problem of the Day, p. 12 Quick Review, p. 12
2 Teach and Practice	Equivalent Fractions, pp. C1–C2, Simplest Form, pp. C3–C4	Mixed Numbers, pp. C5–C6 Adding Like Fractions, pp. C7–C8 Adding Like Mixed Numbers, p. C9 Extra Information, p. C10 Make a Graph, p. C11
3 Extra Practice	Simplest Form, p. P13	Mixed Numbers, p. P14

4 Wrap Up and Assess	**PRETEST**
	 Book C Pretest, pp. 9–10
	    Assess knowledge of fractions
	    and problem solving	

First-Place Math

Fractions

OBJECTIVES (CONTINUED)

SKILLS (CONTINUED)
- To compare unlike fractions
- To find part of a set for a given fraction

PROBLEM SOLVING
- To determine when extra information is given in problems
- To construct a bar graph to solve problems
- To solve problems by choosing the operation
- To make a list to solve problems
- To solve problems by working backwards

DAY 3 pages T70–T75	DAY 4 pages T76–T81	DAY 5 pages T82–T87
WARM-UP RESOURCES Number of the Day, p. 13 Problem of the Day, p. 13 Quick Review, p. 13	**WARM-UP RESOURCES** Number of the Day, p. 14 Problem of the Day, p. 14 Quick Review, p. 14	**WARM-UP RESOURCES** Number of the Day, p. 15 Problem of the Day, p. 15 Quick Review, p. 15
Subtracting Like Fractions, pp. C12–C13 Subtracting Like Mixed Numbers, p. C14 Adding and Subtracting Mixed Numbers, p. C15 Choose the Operation, p. C16 Make a List, p. C17	Adding Like Mixed Numbers, p. C18 Subtracting Like Mixed Numbers, p. C19 Adding and Subtracting Mixed Numbers, p. C20 Adding Unlike Fractions, p. C21 Subtracting Unlike Fractions, p. C22 Work Backwards, p. C23	Comparing Unlike Fractions, p. C24 Finding Parts of Sets, p. C25 Equivalent Fractions, p. C26
It Makes a Difference!, p. P15	Fractions in Flight, p. P16	Finding Parts of Sets, p. P17 Facts Practice, p. P18 Game: *Zoom* 
		WRAP UP Review, p. C27 Home Connection, p. C28 **TEST** Book C Test, pp. 11–12 Assess knowledge of fractions and problem solving

Book C

Week 3

Fractions

DAY 1 At a Glance

Objectives

- To assess knowledge of fractions and problem solving
- To find equivalent fractions
- To write fractions in simplest form

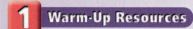

1 Warm-Up Resources

- Number of the Day
- Problem of the Day
- Quick Review

Book C Pretest, pp. 9–10

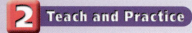

2 Teach and Practice

Book C • Fractions, pp. C1–C4

Manipulatives: Fraction bars

3 Extra Practice

Practice Activities, p. P13

1 Warm-Up Resources

Have students work the following problems. Discuss their strategies and solutions.

Number of the Day

John spent 3 quarters. The number of the day is the fraction of a dollar that he spent. $\frac{75}{100}$ or $\frac{3}{4}$

Problem of the Day

Find fractions of numbers in the classroom. Examples: What fraction of the desks are in the first row? What fraction of the class is boys? What fraction of the class is girls? What fraction of the class is absent? Answers will vary.

Quick Review

Write the fraction for each.

1. one third $\frac{1}{3}$
2. five sixths $\frac{5}{6}$
3. one half $\frac{1}{2}$
4. four fifths $\frac{4}{5}$

Vocabulary

equivalent fractions	two or more fractions that name the same amount (p. C1)
fraction	a number that names a part of a whole or a part of a group (p. C1)
denominator	the part of a fraction that tells how many equal parts are in the whole (p. C2)
numerator	the part of a fraction that tells how many parts of the whole are being considered (p. C2)
simplest form	a fraction is in simplest form when 1 is the only number that can divide evenly into the numerator and the denominator (p. C3)

First-Place Math

Pretest

Have students complete the Pretest (**Assessment**, pp. 9–10) for Book C • Fractions.

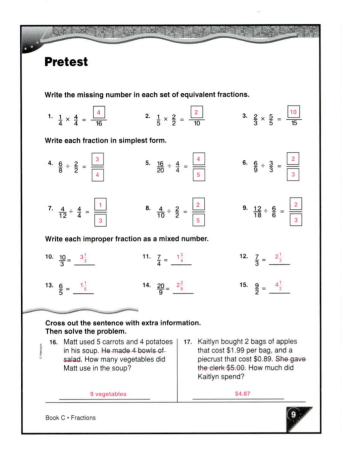
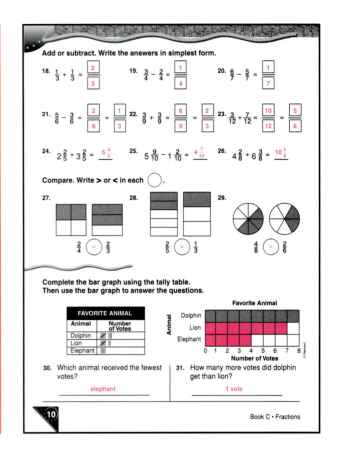

Pretest Items	Skill	Review
1–3	Equivalent Fractions	C1–C2
4–9	Simplest Form	C3–C4
10–15	Mixed Numbers	C5–C6
16–17	Extra Information	C10
18, 22–23	Add Like Fractions	C7–C8
19–21	Subtract Like Fractions	C12–C13
24, 26	Add Like Mixed Numbers	C9, C18
25	Subtract Like Mixed Numbers	C14, C19
27–29	Compare Unlike Fractions	C24
30–31	Make a Graph	C11

Check What Students Know

If a student answers an item incorrectly, refer to the "Review" column to determine where the related skill is taught. You may wish to record students' results on their record forms. (**Assessment**, p. 27)

GO ON

Book C **T59**

2 Teach and Practice

For an introductory activity using fraction bars, see *More Manipulative Activities,* p. T178.

Modeling the Math

Use fraction bars to model the equivalent fractions: $\frac{1}{4} = \frac{2}{8}$. Then have students use fraction bars to work similar problems.

1. Start with one whole bar.

2. Line up a $\frac{1}{4}$ bar with the whole bar.

3. Use $\frac{1}{8}$ bars to match the length of the $\frac{1}{4}$ bar.

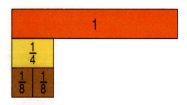

4. Count the number of $\frac{1}{8}$ bars that have the same length as the $\frac{1}{4}$ bar.

Two $\frac{1}{8}$ bars are the same length as one $\frac{1}{4}$ bar.

So, $\frac{1}{4} = \frac{2}{8}$.

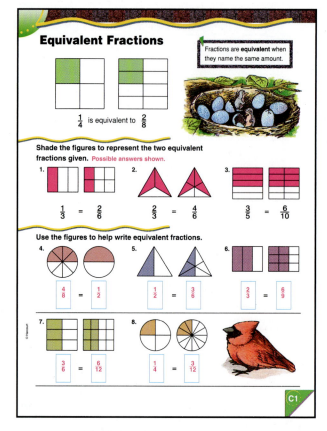

Teach Page C1 Define the vocabulary words for p. C1. Then use fraction bars to model the example exercise, as described in the *Modeling the Math*. Start with the bar for 1. Then line up one $\frac{1}{4}$ bar and two $\frac{1}{8}$ bars. **How can you tell that $\frac{1}{4}$ and $\frac{2}{8}$ are equivalent fractions?** because the $\frac{1}{4}$ bar and the two $\frac{1}{8}$ bars are the same length

Guided Practice Have students solve Exercises 1 and 4. Check students' answers. **Why is the fraction for the first figure in Exercise 4 written as $\frac{4}{8}$ instead of $\frac{1}{2}$?** The circle is divided into 8 equal parts and 4 parts are shaded, so the fraction shown is $\frac{4}{8}$.

Independent Practice Assign Exercises 2–3 and 5–8.

• You may wish to also teach p. C2 before students work independently.

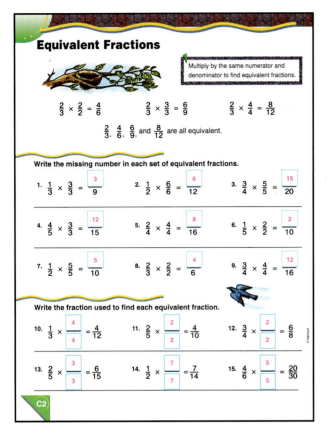
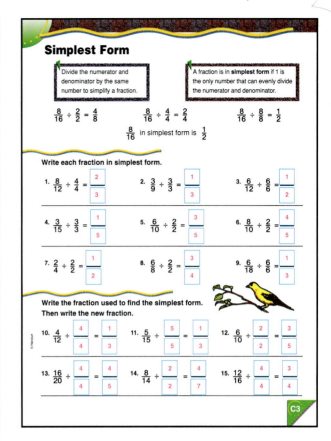

Teach Page C2 Define the vocabulary words for p. C2. Then, use fraction bars to model the example exercise. Start with the bar for 1. Line up fraction bars to show $\frac{2}{3}, \frac{4}{6}, \frac{6}{9},$ and $\frac{8}{12}$.
In the example exercise what is each fraction being multiplied by? Explain.
1; $\frac{2}{2}, \frac{3}{3},$ and $\frac{4}{4}$ are all equivalent to 1.

Guided Practice Have students solve Exercises 1 and 10. Check students' answers.
In Exercise 10 how did you find the missing numerator and denominator? Possible answer: By finding missing factors in basic multiplication facts; $1 \times 4 = 4$ and $3 \times 4 = 12$.

Independent Practice Assign Exercises 2–9 and 11–15.

• After students complete p. C2, continue instruction to teach p. C3.

Teach Page C3 Define the vocabulary word for p. C3. Then, show students how to work the example exercise. **In the example exercise, are the values of the fractions different? Explain.** No; since you are dividing by fractions that are equivalent to 1, the fractions have the same value.

Guided Practice Have students solve Exercise 1. Check students' answers.
In Exercise 1 how do you know that $\frac{2}{3}$ is in simplest form? Possible answer: 1 is the only number that can be divided evenly into the numerator and the denominator.

Independent Practice Assign Exercises 2–15.

• You may wish to also teach p. C4 before students work independently.

Book C T61

3 Extra Practice

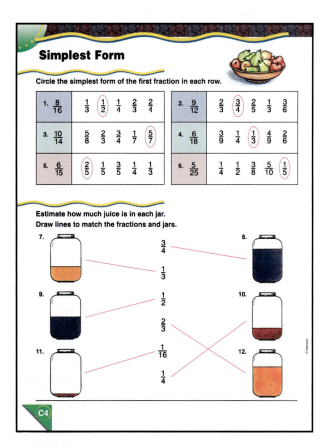

After students complete p. C4, you may wish to assign **Practice Activities**, p. P13.

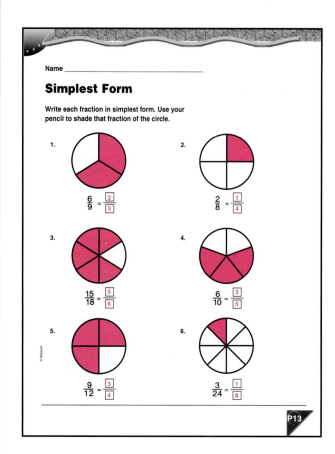

Teach Page C4 Show students how to use division to find the answer to Exercise 1. **Which other fraction is equivalent to $\frac{8}{16}$?** $\frac{2}{4}$ **How do you know that this fraction is not in simplest form?** The numerator and the denominator can each be divided evenly by 2.

Guided Practice Have students solve Exercise 2. Check students' answers. **In Exercise 2 what number can you divide the numerator and the denominator by to find the simplest form of $\frac{9}{12}$?** 3

Independent Practice Assign Exercises 3–12.

First-Place Math

Teaching Notes

Week 3

Fractions

DAY 2 At a Glance

Objectives

- To understand and write mixed numbers
- To add like fractions and express answers in simplest form

Problem Solving

- To determine when extra information is given in problems
- To construct a bar graph to solve problems

1 Warm-Up Resources

- Number of the Day
- Problem of the Day
- Quick Review

2 Teach and Practice

Book C • Fractions, pp. C5–C11

Manipulatives: Fraction bars

3 Extra Practice

Practice Activities, p. P14

T64 First-Place Math

1 Warm-Up Resources

Have students work the following problems. Discuss their strategies and solutions.

Number of the Day

The number of the day is the fraction of the months that have exactly 30 days. Write the fraction in simplest form. $\frac{1}{3}$ of the months have 30 days

Problem of the Day

Megan placed unequal amounts of money in two envelopes. The total amount in the envelopes was $12.00. She gave her brother, Kyle, the envelope that had more money in it. What is the greatest amount and the least amount Kyle could have received? $11.99; $6.01

Quick Review

1. 13 ÷ 2   6r1
2. 27 ÷ 4   6r3
3. 41 ÷ 5   8r1
4. 23 ÷ 3   7r2

Vocabulary

improper fraction — a fraction in which the numerator is greater than the denominator (p. C5)

mixed number — an amount that is made up of a whole number and a fraction (p. C5)

tally sheet — a way to organize data that uses tally marks to show how often something happens (p. C11)

2 Teach and Practice

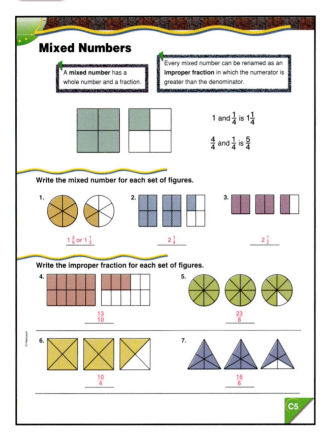

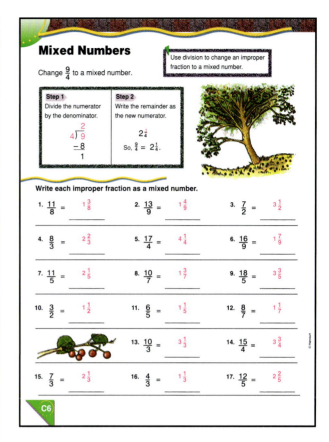

Teach Page C5 Define the vocabulary words for p. C5. Then, use fraction bars to model the example exercise. Line up a whole bar and a $\frac{1}{4}$ bar with five $\frac{1}{4}$ bars. **Do $1\frac{1}{4}$ and $\frac{5}{4}$ have the same value? Explain.** Yes; both sets of fraction bars are the same length, so they have the same value.

Guided Practice Have students solve Exercises 1 and 4. Check students' answers. **How many tenths would it take to make 2 wholes?** 20 tenths

Independent Practice Assign Exercises 2–3 and 5–7.

• You may wish to also teach p. C6 before students work independently.

Teach Page C6 Use fraction bars to model the example exercise. Show nine $\frac{1}{4}$ bars in a row. Have students find how many groups of four $\frac{1}{4}$ bars there are, and how many $\frac{1}{4}$ bars are left over. Connect the model to the step using division. **Why can you use division to change an improper fraction to a mixed number?** Possible answer: Since you want to find how many groups of $\frac{4}{4}$ there are in $\frac{9}{4}$, think $9 \div 4 = 2r1$. The quotient tells how many wholes and the remainder tells how many fractional parts are left over.

Guided Practice Have students solve Exercise 1. Check students' answers. **How do you know whether a fraction is greater than 1?** The numerator is greater than the denominator.

Independent Practice Assign Exercises 2–17.

• After students complete p. C6, continue instruction to teach p. C7.

Book C T65

2 Teach and Practice continued

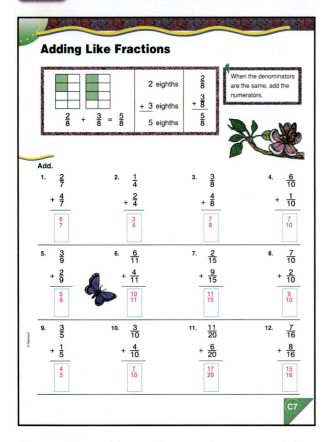

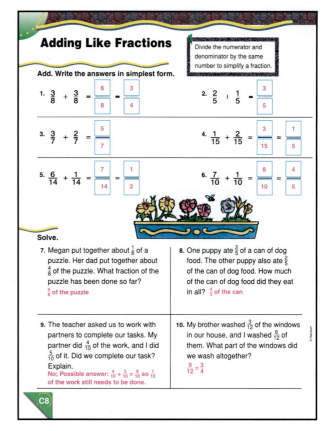

Teach Page C7 Use fraction bars to model the example exercise. Show two $\frac{1}{8}$ bars and three $\frac{1}{8}$ bars. Explain that when you add, you combine the groups of fractions. So, 2 eighths + 3 eighths = 5 eighths. **How do you know $\frac{2}{8}$ and $\frac{3}{8}$ are like fractions?** They have the same denominator.

Guided Practice Have students solve Exercise 1. Check students' answers. **What happens to the numerators and the denominators when you add like fractions?** The numerators are added together and the denominator remains the same.

Independent Practice Assign Exercises 2–12.

● You may wish to also teach p. C8 before students work independently.

Teach Page C8 Use fraction bars to model Exercise 1. Start with a bar for 1. Line up three $\frac{1}{8}$ bars and add three $\frac{1}{8}$ bars. Use $\frac{1}{4}$ bars to show how to model fractions that are equivalent to $\frac{6}{8}$. **Which equivalent fraction shows $\frac{6}{8}$ in simplest form?** $\frac{3}{4}$

Guided Practice Have students solve Exercise 2. Check students' answers. **How do you know $\frac{3}{5}$ is in simplest form?** 1 is the only number that can divide evenly into the numerator and the denominator.

Independent Practice Assign Exercises 3–10.

● After students complete p. C8, continue instruction to teach p. C9.

T66 First-Place Math

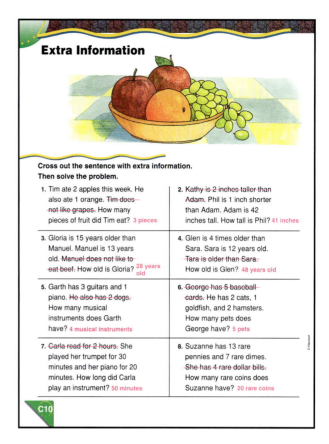

Teach Page C9 Use fraction bars or draw a picture to model the example exercise. Show 3 whole bars and a $\frac{1}{4}$ bar. Then add 2 whole bars and two $\frac{1}{4}$ bars. **How do you add the fractional parts of the mixed numbers?** Since the fractional parts are like, add the numerators and keep the denominator the same. $\frac{1}{4} + \frac{2}{4} = \frac{3}{4}$

Guided Practice Have students solve Exercise 1. Check students' answers. **What are the steps you use to add mixed numbers?** First add the fractions, and then add the whole numbers.

Independent Practice Assign Exercises 2–12. Note that none of the exercises require writing the answer in simplest form.

- After students complete p. C9, continue instruction to teach p. C10.

Teach Page C10 Write each sentence of Problem 1 on the board. Discuss what is being asked. Decide what information is needed to solve the problem. **Which sentence has information that is not needed to solve the problem?** Tim does not like grapes. Then solve the problem.

Guided Practice Have students solve Problem 2. Check students' work. **Why is it important to find extra information in a problem?** Possible answer: If there is extra information, it should not be used when solving the problem.

Independent Practice Assign Problems 3–8.

- After students complete p. C10, continue instruction to teach p. C11.

Book C T67

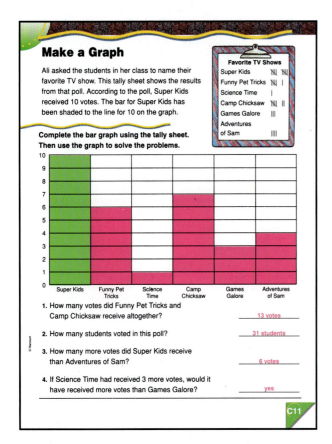

Teach Page C11 Define the vocabulary word for p. C11. Then, use the data on the tally sheet to complete the bar for Funny Pet Tricks. **What do the numbers on the left side of the graph represent?** the number of votes

Guided Practice Have students complete the bar graph. Check students' graphs. **What is the interval for this bar graph?** 1 Have students solve Problem 1. Check students' answers.

Independent Practice Assign Problems 2–4.

After students complete p. C11, you may wish to assign **Practice Activities**, p. P14.

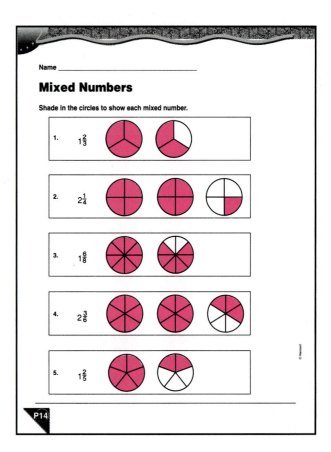

T68 First-Place Math

Teaching Notes

Week 3

Fractions

DAY 3 At a Glance

Objectives

- To subtract like fractions
- To add and subtract mixed numbers

Problem Solving

- To solve problems by choosing the operation
- To make a list to solve problems

1 Warm-Up Resources

- Number of the Day
- Problem of the Day
- Quick Review

page 13

2 Teach and Practice

Book C • Fractions, pp. C12–C17

Manipulatives: Fraction bars

3 Extra Practice

Practice Activities, p. P15

T70 First-Place Math

---

1 Warm-Up Resources

Have students work the following problems. Discuss their strategies and solutions.

Number of the Day

Write three equivalent fractions that represent 40 minutes as a fraction of an hour. **Possible answer:** $\frac{40}{60}$, $\frac{4}{6}$, or $\frac{2}{3}$.

Problem of the Day

Matt, Ron, and Greg each had a small pizza for lunch. One ate $\frac{2}{3}$ of his pizza, another ate $\frac{3}{4}$ of his pizza, and the other ate $\frac{1}{2}$ of his pizza. Matt ate the most. Ron had the most left. How much did each person eat? **Matt ate $\frac{3}{4}$ of his pizza; Greg ate $\frac{2}{3}$ of his pizza; Ron ate $\frac{1}{2}$ of his pizza.**

Quick Review

Find the simplest form.

1. $\frac{3}{6}$ $\frac{1}{2}$
2. $\frac{14}{21}$ $\frac{2}{3}$
3. $\frac{6}{24}$ $\frac{1}{4}$
4. $\frac{8}{40}$ $\frac{1}{5}$

Vocabulary

simplest form a fraction is in simplest form when 1 is the only number that can divide evenly into the numerator and the denominator (p. C13)

2 Teach and Practice

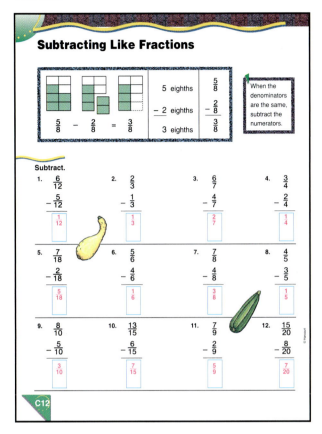

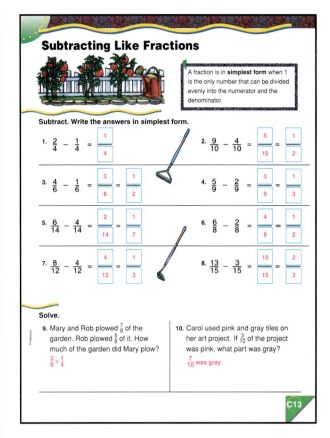

Teach Page C12 Use fraction bars to model the example exercise. Show five $\frac{1}{8}$ bars and take away two $\frac{1}{8}$ bars. After completing the exercise, ask, **How can you use addition to check the difference?** Add $\frac{2}{8}$ and $\frac{3}{8}$ to get $\frac{5}{8}$.

Guided Practice Have students solve Exercise 1. Check students' answers. **How is subtracting like fractions similar to adding like fractions?** Possible answer: you add or subtract the numerators and the denominators stay the same.

Independent Practice Assign Exercises 2–12.

• You may wish to also teach p. C13 before students work independently.

Teach Page C13 Define the vocabulary word for p. C13. Then, use fraction bars to model Exercises 1 and 2. Use take away and comparison methods of subtracting. For Exercise 2, use fraction bars to model equivalent fractions. **Which equivalent fraction shows $\frac{5}{10}$ in simplest form?** $\frac{1}{2}$

Guided Practice Have students solve Exercise 3. Check students' answers. **If two fractions are in simplest form, will the difference between them be in simplest form? Give an example.** Not always; possible example: $\frac{7}{12} - \frac{5}{12} = \frac{2}{12}$ or $\frac{1}{6}$.

Independent Practice Assign Exercises 4–10.

• After students complete p. C13, continue instruction to teach p. C14.

GO ON

Book C T71

2 Teach and Practice continued

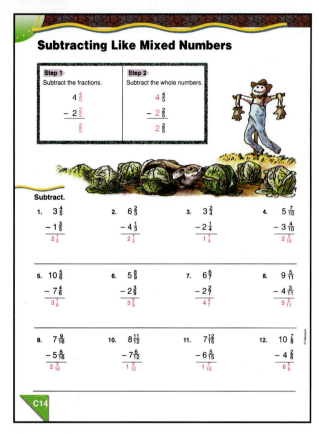

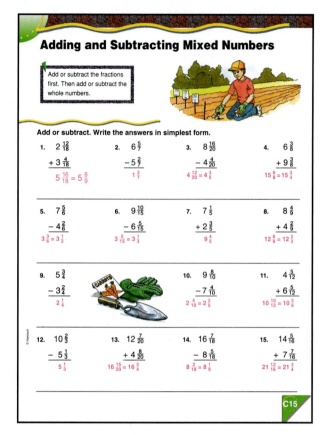

Teach Page C14 Use fraction bars to model the example exercise. Show 4 whole bars and four $\frac{1}{5}$ bars. First take away two $\frac{1}{5}$ bars, and then take away 2 whole bars. Connect the use of the fraction bars to the steps in the example. **How can you check the answer?** Possible answer: Add the difference to the amount subtracted to get the original amount.

Guided Practice Have students solve Exercise 1. Check students' answers. **What are the steps used to subtract mixed numbers?** First subtract the fractional parts, and then subtract the whole numbers.

Independent Practice Assign Exercises 2–12.

- After students complete p. C14, continue instruction to teach p. C15.

Teach Page C15 Explain how to solve Exercises 1 and 2. First add or subtract the fractions, and then add or subtract the whole numbers. Check that the sum or difference is in simplest form. **How can you tell if a mixed number is in simplest form?** Possible answer: Look at the fractional part of the mixed number. If the numerator and the denominator can only be divided evenly by 1, then the mixed number is in simplest form.

Guided Practice Have students solve Exercise 3. Check students' answers. **What number can you divide the numerator and the denominator by to find the simplest form?** 4

Independent Practice Assign Exercises 4–15.

- After students complete p. C15, continue instruction to teach p. C16.

T72 First-Place Math

Teaching Notes

Week 3

Fractions

DAY 4 At a Glance

Objectives

- To add and subtract like mixed numbers and record the answer in simplest form
- To add and subtract unlike fractions using models

Problem Solving

- To solve problems by working backwards

1 Warm-Up Resources

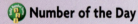
- Number of the Day
- Problem of the Day
- Quick Review

 page 14

2 Teach and Practice

Book C • Fractions, pp. C18–C23

Manipulatives:
  Fraction bars
  Two-color counters

3 Extra Practice

Practice Activities, p. P16

---

1 Warm-Up Resources

Have students work the following problems. Discuss their strategies and solutions.

 ### Number of the Day

Write two equivalent fractions using 4 as the numerator in one fraction and 4 as the denominator in the other fraction. **Possible answer:** $\frac{4}{8}, \frac{2}{4}$

 ### Problem of the Day

Complete the Magic Square. The magic square sum is $1\frac{7}{8}$.

1	$\frac{1}{8}$	$\frac{6}{8}$
$\frac{3}{8}$	$\frac{5}{8}$	$\frac{7}{8}$
$\frac{4}{8}$	$1\frac{1}{8}$	$\frac{2}{8}$

 ### Quick Review

1. $\frac{6}{10} - \frac{2}{10}$ $\frac{4}{10}$, or $\frac{2}{5}$
2. $\frac{6}{14} + \frac{2}{14}$ $\frac{8}{14}$, or $\frac{4}{7}$
3. $6\frac{5}{8} - 3\frac{3}{8}$ $3\frac{2}{8}$, or $3\frac{1}{4}$
4. $4\frac{1}{4} + 3\frac{1}{4} = 7\frac{2}{4}$ or $7\frac{1}{2}$

Vocabulary

mixed number an amount that is made up of a whole number and a fraction (p. C18)

T76 First-Place Math

2 Teach and Practice

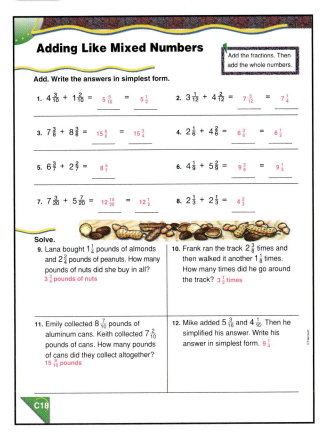

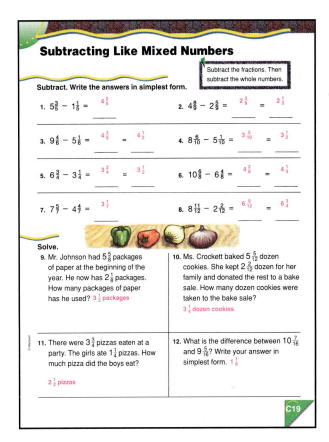

Teach Page C18 Define the vocabulary word for p. C18. Then, use fraction bars or draw pictures to model Exercise 1. First add the fractions, and then add the whole numbers. **How do you know that $5\frac{5}{10}$ is not in simplest form?** because the numerator and the denominator of the fractional part can each be divided evenly by 5

Guided Practice Have students solve Exercise 2. Check students' answers. **What number can you divide the numerator and the denominator by to find the simplest form?** 3

Independent Practice Assign Exercises 3–12.

- After students complete p. C18, continue instruction to teach p. C19.

Teach Page C19 Use fraction bars or draw pictures to model Exercise 1. Show $5\frac{3}{5}$ and then take away $1\frac{1}{5}$. **How can you use fraction bars to model the comparison method of subtraction?** Possible answer: Line up $5\frac{3}{5}$ and $1\frac{1}{5}$. First compare the fractional parts, and then compare the whole numbers.

Guided Practice Have students solve Exercise 2. Check students' answers. **How do you know that the difference is not in simplest form?** because the numerator and the denominator of the fraction can each be divided evenly by 3

Independent Practice Assign Exercises 3–12.

- You may wish to also teach p. C20 before students work independently.

Book C T77

2 Teach and Practice continued

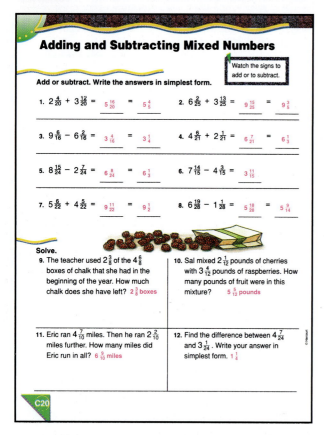

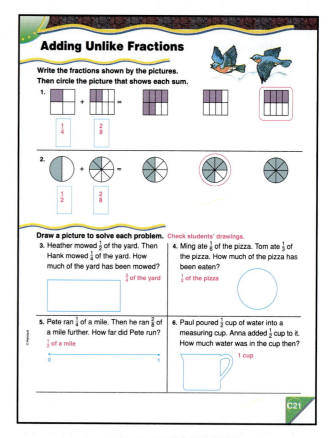

Teach Page C20 Write Exercise 1 on the board vertically. Add the fractional parts first, and then add the whole numbers. **What number can be evenly divided into both the numerator and the denominator to find the simplest form?** 4

Guided Practice Have students solve Exercise 2. Check students' answers. **How did you know which operation to use for this exercise?** The plus sign means that it is an addition exercise.

Independent Practice Assign Exercises 3–12.

● After students complete p. C20, continue instruction to teach p. C21.

Teach Page C21 Use fraction bars to model Exercise 1. Start with one whole bar. Line up a bar for $\frac{1}{4}$ and add two $\frac{1}{8}$ bars. Use $\frac{1}{8}$ bars to find the fraction that is equivalent to the sum, $\frac{4}{8}$. **Why can't you add the numerators of each fraction to find the sum?** Fourths and eighths are different sizes, so the fractions are not alike. For exercises 3–6, it may be helpful for students to use the fraction strips found on p. C29.

Guided Practice Have students solve Exercise 2. Check students' answers. **How is adding unlike fractions different from adding like fractions?** Possible answer: When fractions have different denominators, you cannot add the numerators and keep the denominators the same.

Independent Practice Assign Exercises 3–6.

● After students complete p. C21, continue instruction to teach p. C22.

T78 First-Place Math

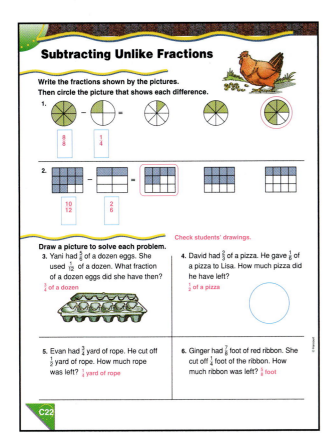
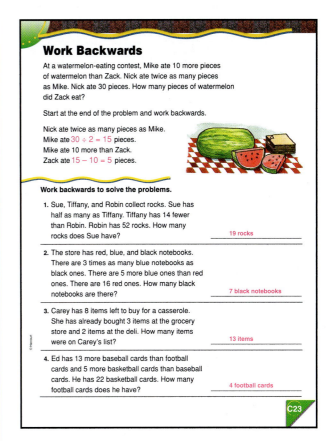

Teach Page C22 Use fraction bars to model Exercise 1. Start with one whole bar. Line up eight $\frac{1}{8}$ bars, and under those, line up a $\frac{1}{4}$ bar. Compare the bars, and use $\frac{1}{8}$ bars to fit the difference. **Why should the $\frac{1}{4}$ bar be placed under the eight $\frac{1}{8}$ bars?** Since you are subtracting $\frac{1}{4}$ from $\frac{8}{8}$, you place it underneath so you can compare to find the difference.

Guided Practice Have students solve Exercise 2. Check students' answers. **How can you use the take-away method to subtract unlike fractions?** Possible answer: First find an equivalent fraction that uses like fractions, and then take away like fractions.

Independent Practice Assign Exercises 3–6.

• After students complete p. C22, continue instruction to teach p. C23.

Teach Page C23 Use counters to model the example problem. Explain that since you know how many pieces Nick ate, you start there. **What operations were used to solve this problem?** division and subtraction

Guided Practice Have students solve Problem 1. Check students' work. **What part of the problem did you solve first?** Tiffany has 52 − 14, or 38, rocks. **second?** Sue has 38 ÷ 2, or 19, rocks.

Independent Practice Assign Problems 2–4.

3 Extra Practice

After students complete p. C23, you may wish to assign **Practice Activities**, p. P16.

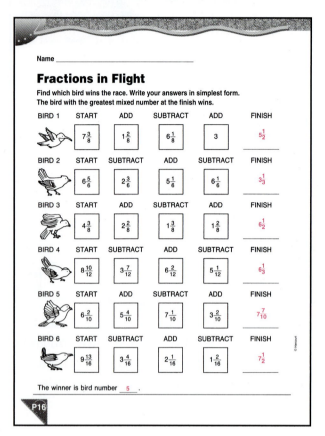

Teaching Notes

T80 First-Place Math

Teaching Notes

Week 3

Fractions

DAY 5
At a Glance

Objectives
- To compare unlike fractions
- To find part of a set for a given fraction
- To assess knowledge of fractions and problem solving

1 Warm-Up Resources
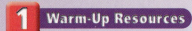
- Number of the Day
- Problem of the Day
- Quick Review

page 15

2 Teach and Practice

Book C • Fractions, pp. C24–C26

Manipulatives:
  Fraction circles
  Two-color counters
  Fraction bars

3 Extra Practice

Practice Activities, pp. P17–P18
Game: Zoom

Manipulatives:
  Color tiles

4 Wrap Up and Assess

Fractions Review, p. C27
Home Connection, p. C28
Book C Test, pp. 11–12

T82 First-Place Math

---

1 Warm-Up Resources

Have students work the following problems. Discuss their strategies and solutions.

Number of the Day

Write the number of hours you slept last night as a fraction of a day. **Possible answer: 8 hours; $\frac{8}{24}$, or $\frac{1}{3}$, of a day**

Problem of the Day

The letters A, B, C, and D represent the digits 1, 2, 3, and 4, but not in that order. Use the digits for the letters to make a correct equation. $\frac{AB}{B} = C\frac{D}{B} = C\frac{A}{D}$

If A = 1, B = 4, C = 3, D = 2, then $\frac{14}{4} = 3\frac{2}{4} = 3\frac{1}{2}$

Quick Review

1. $\frac{6}{10} - \frac{2}{10}$ $\frac{4}{10}$, or $\frac{2}{5}$
2. $\frac{10}{12} - \frac{3}{12}$ $\frac{7}{12}$
3. $\frac{10}{15} - \frac{9}{15}$ $\frac{1}{15}$
4. $\frac{8}{9} - \frac{2}{9}$ $\frac{6}{9}$, or $\frac{2}{3}$

Vocabulary

Review the vocabulary for Week 3.

equivalent fractions	two or more fractions that name the same amount (p. C1)
fraction	a number that names a part of a whole or a part of a group (p. C1)
denominator	the part of a fraction that tells how many equal parts are in the whole (p. C2)
numerator	the part of a fraction that tells how many parts of the whole are being considered (p. C2)
improper fraction	a fraction in which the numerator is greater than the denominator (p. C5)
mixed number	an amount that is made up of a whole number and a fraction (p. C5)

2 Teach and Practice

For an introductory activity using fraction circles, see *More Manipulative Activities*, p. T179.

Modeling the Math

Use fraction circles to compare $\frac{1}{4}$ and $\frac{2}{6}$. Then have students use fraction circles to work similar problems.

1. Start with the circle for 1 whole.

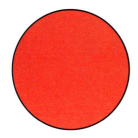

2. Show a $\frac{1}{4}$ piece.

3. Show two $\frac{1}{6}$ pieces.

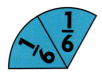

4. Compare the fractions. Place the $\frac{1}{4}$ piece on top of the two $\frac{1}{6}$ pieces to check.

So, $\frac{1}{4} < \frac{2}{6}$.

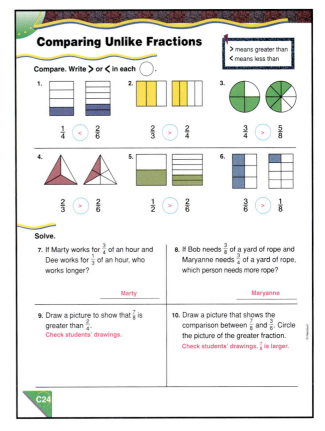

Teach Page C24 Use fraction circles to model Exercise 1, as described in the *Modeling the Math*. **How do you know which fraction is greater?** by comparing the portion of each circle that is described by the fractions

Guided Practice Have students solve Exercise 2. Check students' answers. **What do you notice about the numerators and the denominators of these fractions and how the fractions compare?** Possible answer: The numerators are the same, but the denominators are different. Since thirds are greater than fourths, $\frac{2}{3}$ is greater than $\frac{2}{4}$.

Independent Practice Assign Exercises 3–10.

- After students complete p. C24, continue instruction to teach p. C25.

Book C T83

2 Teach and Practice continued

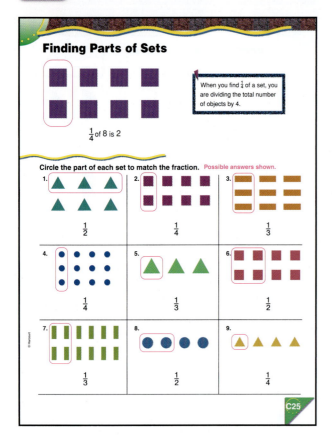

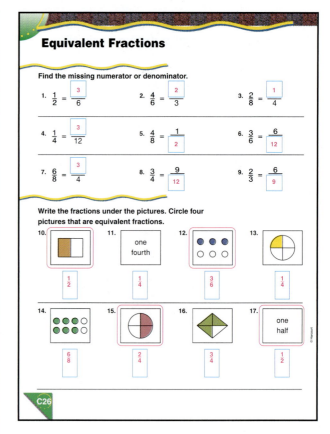

Teach Page C25 Use counters to model the example exercise. Show a set of 8 counters. Explain that when you find a fractional part of a set, you divide the set into equal groups. Separate the counters into 4 equal groups. **How many counters are in each group?** 2 **What would be $\frac{3}{4}$ of 8?** 6

Guided Practice Have students solve Exercise 1. Check students' answers. **What number do you divide a set by to find $\frac{1}{2}$ of the set?** 2

Independent Practice Assign Exercises 2–9.

● After students complete p. C25, continue instruction to teach p. C26.

Teach Page C26 Use fraction bars to model Exercise 1. Start with one whole bar. Line up a $\frac{1}{2}$ bar. Use $\frac{1}{6}$ bars to find an equivalent fraction. **How do you know to use $\frac{1}{6}$ bars to solve this exercise?** The denominator of the equivalent fraction is 6.

Guided Practice Have students solve Exercise 2. Check students' answers. **In Exercise 2 do you use multiplication or division to find the equivalent fraction? Explain.** Division; divide the numerator and the denominator by 2 to find the equivalent fraction in thirds.

Independent Practice Assign Exercises 3–17.

First-Place Math

3 Extra Practice

After students complete p. C26, you may wish to assign **Practice Activities**, pp. P17–P18.

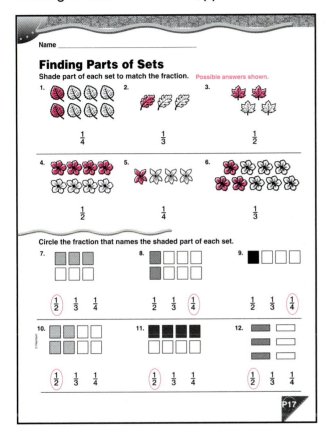

- You may also wish to have students play the game *Zoom* to practice fractions.

4 Wrap Up and Assess

Have students complete p. C27 to prepare for the Test.

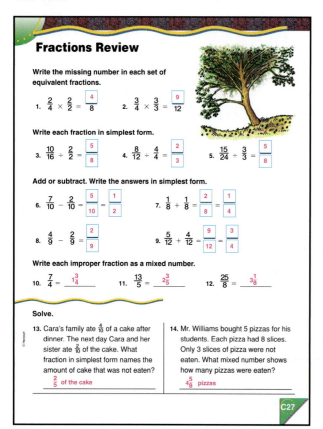

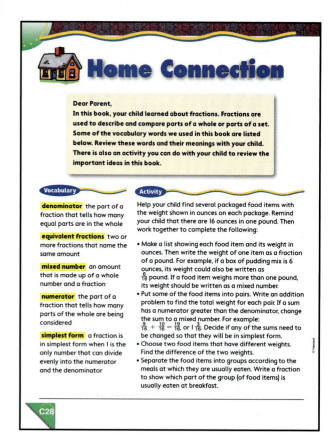

Use the following information to determine which pages students should review before taking the Book C Test.

Review Items	Skill	Review
1–2	Equivalent Fractions	C1–C2
3–5, 13	Simplest Form	C3–C4
6, 8	Subtract Like Fractions	C12–C13
7, 9	Add Like Fractions	C7–C8
10–12, 14	Mixed Numbers	C5–C6

Review the Home Connection page with students. You may want to preview the activity with students so they can explain it to their parents.

First-Place Math

Test

Have students complete the Test (Assessment, pp. 11–12) for Book C • Fractions.

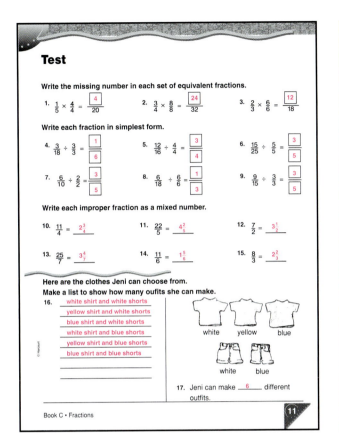
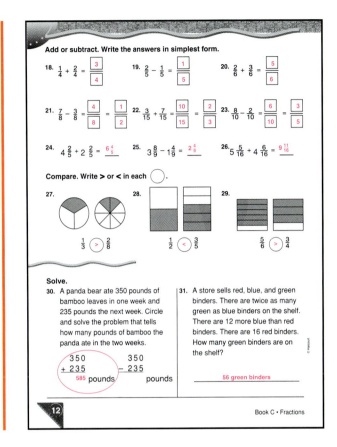

Test Items	Skill	Review
1–3	Equivalent Fractions	C1–C2
4–9	Simplest Form	C3–C4
10–15	Mixed Numbers	C5–C6
16–17	Make a List	C17
18, 20, 22	Add Like Fractions	C7–C8
19, 21, 23	Subtract Like Fractions	C12–C13
24, 26	Add Like Mixed Numbers	C9, C18
25	Subtract Like Mixed Numbers	C14, C19
27–29	Compare Unlike Fractions	C24
30	Choose the Operation	C16
31	Work Backwards	C23

Check What Students Know

If a student answers an item incorrectly, refer to the "Review" column to determine where the related skill is taught. You may wish to record students' results on their record forms. (**Assessment**, p. 27)

Week 4 Planner

OBJECTIVES
SKILLS
- To compare and order decimals
- To add decimals
- To subtract decimals
- To add and subtract decimals to hundredths
- To add and subtract money

	DAY 1 pages T90–T95	**DAY 2** pages T96–T101
1 Warm-Up	**WARM-UP RESOURCES** Number of the Day, p. 16 Problem of the Day, p. 16 Quick Review, p. 16	**WARM-UP RESOURCES** Number of the Day, p. 17 Problem of the Day, p. 17 Quick Review, p. 17
2 Teach and Practice	Comparing and Ordering Decimals, pp. D1–D2 Adding Decimals, pp. D3–D4	Adding Decimals, pp. D5–D8 Extra Information, p. D9 Too Little Information, p. D10
3 Extra Practice	Decimals Less Than 1, p. P19	Adding Decimals, p. P20
4 Wrap Up and Assess	**PRETEST** Book D Pretest, pp. 13–14 Assess knowledge of decimals and problem solving	

First-Place Math

OBJECTIVES (CONTINUED)
PROBLEM SOLVING
- To determine when extra information is given in problems
- To determine when there is not enough information given to solve a problem
- To make a table to solve problems
- To solve problems using multiple steps
- To solve problems using guess and check

Decimals

DAY 3
pages T102–T107

WARM-UP RESOURCES
Number of the Day, p. 18
Problem of the Day, p. 18
Quick Review, p. 18

Subtracting Decimals, pp. D11–D14
Make a Table, p. D15
Multi-Step Problems, p. D16
Mixed Practice, p. D17

Subtracting Decimals, p. P21

DAY 4
pages T108–T113

WARM-UP RESOURCES
Number of the Day, p. 19
Problem of the Day, p. 19
Quick Review, p. 19

Subtracting Decimals, pp. D18–D19
Guess and Check, p. D20
Mixed Practice, pp. D21–D23

Count On, p. P22

DAY 5
pages T114–T119

WARM-UP RESOURCES
Number of the Day, p. 20
Problem of the Day, p. 20
Quick Review, p. 20

Adding and Subtracting Money, pp. D24–D26

Adding and Subtracting Money, p. P23
Facts Practice, p. P24

Game: *Hoop Time*

WRAP UP
Review, p. D27
Home Connection, p. D28

TEST
Book D Test, pp. 15–16
  Assess knowledge of decimals and problem solving

Book D T89

Week 4

Decimals
DAY 1 At a Glance

Objectives
- To assess knowledge of decimals and problem solving
- To compare and order decimals
- To add decimals

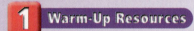
- Number of the Day
- Problem of the Day
- Quick Review

Book D Pretest, pp. 13–14

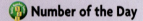

Book D • Decimals, pp. D1–D4

Manipulatives:
 Decimal models

Practice Activities, p. P19

1 Warm-Up Resources

Have students work the following problems. Discuss their strategies and solutions.

Number of the Day
Determine the amount of money the class would have if each person had $0.10. **Answers will vary.**

Problem of the Day
Which number does not belong with the others? Explain. **Possible answers given.**

1. 8, 4, 10, 20, 3, 6 **3; it is the only number that is not an even number**

2. $\frac{2}{3}, \frac{9}{6}, \frac{4}{5}, \frac{1}{2}, \frac{6}{10}$ **$\frac{9}{6}$; it is the only improper fraction**

Quick Review **Possible answer given.**

Write an equivalent fraction.

1. $\frac{2}{4}$ $\frac{1}{2}$
2. $\frac{2}{3}$ $\frac{4}{6}$
3. $\frac{3}{9}$ $\frac{1}{3}$
4. $\frac{4}{6}$ $\frac{2}{3}$

Vocabulary

decimal — a number with one or more digits to the right of the decimal point (p. D1)

decimal point — the mark in a decimal number that separates the ones and the tenths places (p. D4)

First-Place Math

Pretest

Have students complete the Pretest (Assessment, pp. 13–14) for Book D • Decimals.

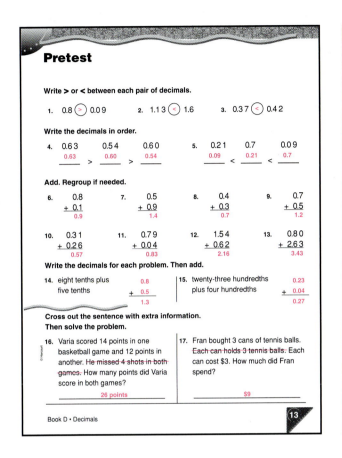
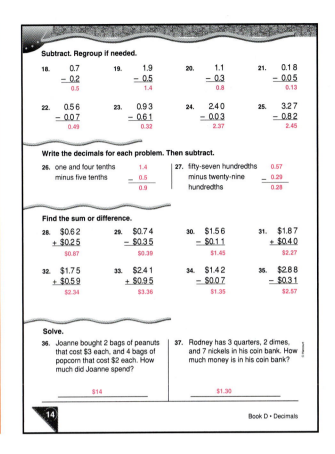

Pretest Items	Skill	Review
1–5	Compare and Order Decimals	D1–D2
6–15	Add Decimals	D3–D8
16–17	Extra Information	D9
18–27	Subtract Decimals	D18–D19
28–35	Add and Subtract Money	D24–D26
36–37	Multi-Step Problems	D16

Check What Students Know

If a student answers an item incorrectly, refer to the "Review" column to determine where the related skill is taught. You may wish to record students' results on their record forms. (**Assessment**, p. 28)

Book D • T91

2 Teach and Practice

For an introductory activity using decimal models, see *More Manipulative Activities*, p. T180.

Modeling the Math

Use decimal models to compare 0.2 and 0.6. Then have students use decimal models to work similar problems.

1. Shade 2 tenths of a decimal model.

2. Shade 6 tenths of another decimal model.

3. Compare the shaded areas of the two decimal models.

    0.2   0.6

The decimal model for 2 tenths has a smaller shaded area than the decimal model for 6 tenths.

So, 0.2 < 0.6.

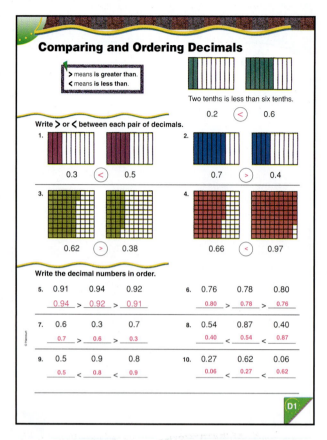

Teach Page D1 Define the vocabulary word for p. D1. Then, use decimal models, found on page D29, to model the example exercise, as described in the *Modeling the Math*. **How can you use what you know about fractions to compare these decimals?** 0.2 is equivalent to $\frac{2}{10}$ and 0.6 is equivalent to $\frac{6}{10}$. Since $\frac{2}{10} < \frac{6}{10}$, then 0.2 < 0.6.

Guided Practice Have students solve Exercise 5. Check students' answers. **How do you know which decimal to list first?** Since the first decimal should be greater than the other two decimals, 0.94 should be first.

Independent Practice Assign Exercises 1–4 and 6–10.

• You may wish to also teach p. D2 before students work independently.

First-Place Math

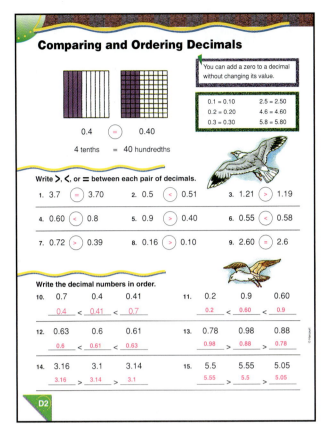
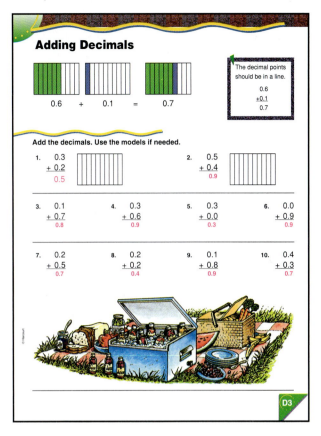

Teach Page D2 Use decimal models, such as those found on p. D29, to demonstrate the example exercise as well as Exercises 1 and 2. **How can you use place-value to compare 0.5 and 0.51?** Think: 0.5 = 0.50. Compare each digit, beginning with the greatest place-value. Ones: 0 = 0; tenths: 5 = 5; hundredths: 0 < 1. So, 0.5 < 0.51.

Guided Practice Have students solve Exercises 3 and 10. Check students' answers. **Why do you compare digits from left to right?** Compare the digits starting with the greatest place-value first.

Independent Practice Assign Exercises 4–9 and 11–15.

- After students complete p. D2, continue instruction to teach p. D3.

Teach Page D3 Discuss the example exercise with students. Direct students' attention to Exercise 1. **Why must the decimal points be lined up when writing the problem vertically?** so that numbers in the same place-value position are in the same column

Guided Practice Have students solve Exercise 1. Check students' answers. **How is adding decimals like adding whole numbers?** They are alike in that you line up place-values and add from right to left. **How is it different?** They are different in that you use a decimal point to separate the whole number part from the decimal part.

Independent Practice Assign Exercises 2–10.

- You may wish to also teach p. D4 before students work independently.

Book D T93

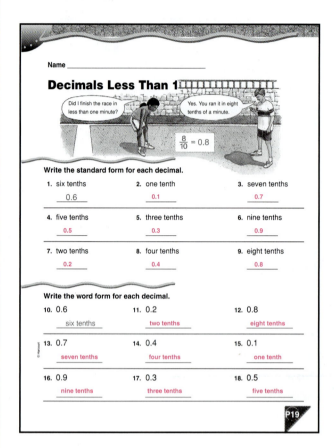

After students complete p. D4, you may wish to assign **Practice Activities,** p. P19.

Teach Page D4 Define the vocabulary word for p. D4. Then, use decimal models, such as those found on p. D29, to demonstrate the example exercise. Shade 3 tenths in one color and begin to shade 9 tenths in another color. When 1 whole is filled, shade the remaining tenths on a second model. **When do you need to regroup when adding tenths?** when the sum of the tenths is 10 or greater

Guided Practice Have students solve Exercise 1. Check students' answers. **Did you need to regroup to solve Exercise 1?** Yes; there were 10 tenths that were regrouped as 1.

Independent Practice Assign Exercises 2–14.

Teaching Notes

Week 4

Decimals

DAY 2 At a Glance

Objectives
- To add decimals

Problem Solving
- To determine when extra information is given in problems
- To determine when there is not enough information given to solve a problem

1 Warm-Up Resources

- 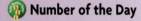 Number of the Day
- 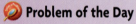 Problem of the Day
- 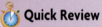 Quick Review

page 17

2 Teach and Practice

Book D • Decimals, pp. D5–D10

Manipulatives: Decimal models

3 Extra Practice

Practice Activities, p. P20

---

1 Warm-Up Resources

Have students work the following problems. Discuss their strategies and solutions.

Number of the Day
Find the number of days in 3 weeks. If Mary worked on her science project 24 days, how many days more or less than three weeks did she work? **3 days more**

Problem of the Day
Christina has one box that weighs 14.8 pounds and another box that weighs 27.2 pounds. What would be the weight of a third box if the total weight of the three boxes is 70 pounds? **28 pounds**

Quick Review
Round each to the nearest ten.

1. 342 **340**
2. 509 **510**
3. 38 **40**
4. 784 **780**

Vocabulary

tenth	one of ten equal parts (p. D6)
hundredth	one of one hundred equal parts (p. D6)

T96 First-Place Math

2 Teach and Practice

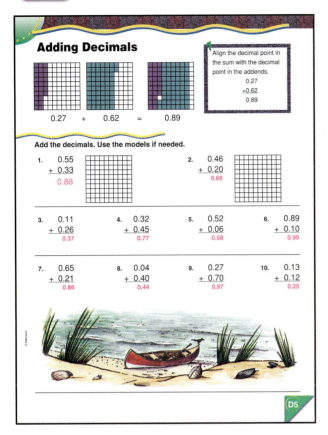

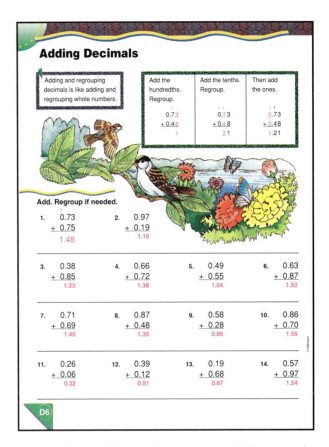

Teach Page D5 Discuss the example exercise with students. **What decimal does one small square of the decimal model show?** 0.01 Discuss how to align the addends before finding the sum.

Guided Practice Have students solve Exercise 1. Check students' answers. **Why is the answer 0.88 instead of 88?** Since you are adding hundredths, 55 hundredths + 33 hundredths = 88 hundredths, or 0.88.

Independent Practice Assign Exercises 2–10. Note that none of the exercises require regrouping.

- You may wish to also teach p. D6 before students work independently.

Teach Page D6 Define the vocabulary words for p. D6. Then, use grid paper to model each step of the example exercise. **How is adding decimals like adding whole numbers?** You line up like place-values and add from right to left, regrouping when necessary. **How is it different?** Since you are adding amounts less than 1, you need to include a decimal point.

Guided Practice Have students solve Exercises 1 and 2. Checks students' answers. **How can you tell without adding that the sums on this page will be less than 2?** Since both addends are less than 1, the sum must be less than 2.

Independent Practice Assign Exercises 3–14.

- You may wish to also teach p. D7 before students work independently.

Book D T97

2 Teach and Practice continued

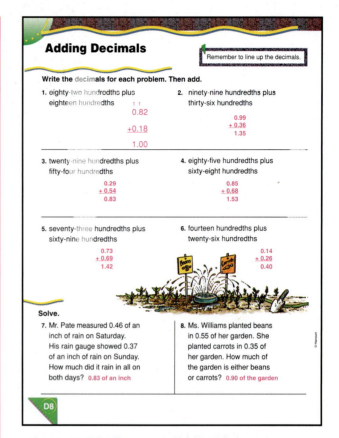

Teach Page D7 Use a place-value chart or grid paper to record Exercise 1. **Why is it important to line up the decimal points?** so you can add like place-values together

Guided Practice Have students solve Exercise 2. Check students' answers. **How do you know whether you need to regroup?** 3 tenths + 8 tenths = 11 tenths. Since 10 tenths, or $\frac{10}{10}$, is equal to 1, 11 tenths should be regrouped as 1 and 1 tenth.

Independent Practice Assign Exercises 3–8. Note that all exercises require regrouping 10 tenths as 1.

- You may wish to also teach p. D8 before students work independently.

Teach Page D8 Use a place-value chart or grid paper to record Exercise 1. **What do the small 1's above the tenths and ones columns show?** 10 hundredths regrouped as 1 tenth, and 10 tenths regrouped as 1.

Guided Practice Have students solve Exercise 2. Check students' answers. **In Exercise 2, how can you use mental math to find the sum?** Possible answer: Since 0.99 + 0.01 = 1 and 0.36 − 0.01 = 0.35, the sum is 1.35.

Independent Practice Assign Exercises 3–8.

- After students complete p. D8, continue instruction to teach p. D9.

T98 First-Place Math

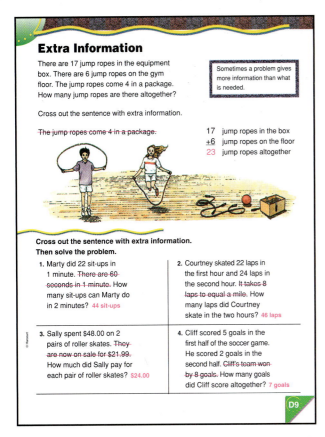

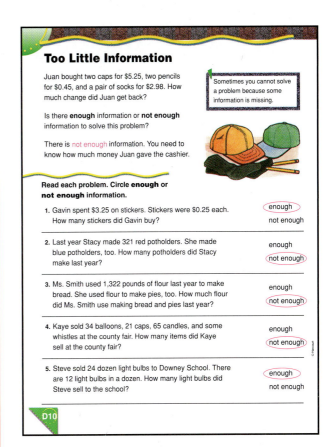

Teach Page D9 Write on the board each sentence of the example problem. Discuss what the problem asks to find and what information is needed to solve it. **Why don't you need to know the number of jump ropes in a package?** There are no packages of jump ropes in the problem. Then solve the problem.

Guided Practice Have students solve Problem 1. Check students' work. **Why is it important to identify extra information in a problem?** Possible answer: so that you don't use the extra information to solve the problem

Independent Practice Assign Problems 2–4.

- You may wish to also teach p. D10 before students work independently.

Teach Page D10 Discuss the question in the example problem. Decide what information is needed to answer the question. **What sentence could be added to the problem so that there would be enough information to solve it?** Possible answer: Juan gave the cashier $10.00 to pay for the caps, pencils, and socks.

Guided Practice Have students read Problem 1 and decide whether there is or isn't enough information to solve it. **How can you solve this problem?** Possible answer: by using play money to find how many groups of 25 cents there are in $3.25

Independent Practice Assign Problems 2–5.

Book D T99

3 Extra Practice

After students complete p. D10, you may wish to assign **Practice Activities**, p. P20.

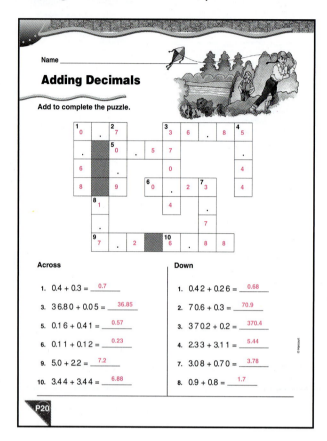

T100 First-Place Math

Teaching Notes

Week 4

Decimals

DAY 3
At a Glance

Objectives
- To subtract decimals
- To add and subtract decimals

Problem Solving
- To make a table to solve problems
- To solve problems using multiple steps

1 Warm-Up Resources
- Number of the Day
- Problem of the Day
- Quick Review

Daily Warm-Up Flip Chart, page 18

2 Teach and Practice

Book D • Decimals, pp. D11–D17

Manipulatives:
 Decimal models
 Two-color counters

3 Extra Practice

Practice Activities, p. P21

---

1 Warm-Up Resources

Have students work the following problems. Discuss their strategies and solutions.

Number of the Day

Using the digits 1–9, write two decimal numbers that have a sum of 6.1. **Possible answer: 1.7 and 4.4**

Problem of the Day

The value of each of two decimal numbers is less than 0.5. Each decimal has a 5 or 0 in the hundredths place. In the greater number, the digit in the hundredths place is 1 more than the digit in the tenths place. In the lesser number, the digit in the tenths place is 3 more than the digit in the hundredths place. What are the two numbers? **0.45 and 0.30**

Quick Review

1. 125 − 28 = ___ **97**
2. 1,085 − 928 = ___ **157**
3. 3,518 − 473 = ___ **3,045**
4. 5,376 − 2,654 = ___ **2,722**

Vocabulary

decimal — a number with one or more digits to the right of the decimal point (p. D11)

decimal point — the mark in a decimal number that separates the ones and the tenths places (p. D11)

T102 First-Place Math

2 Teach and Practice

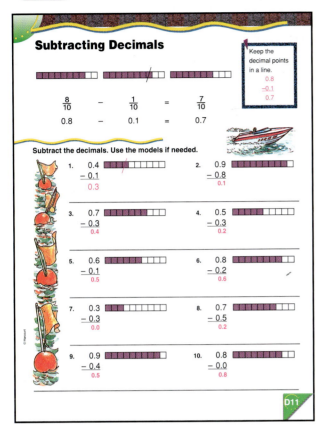

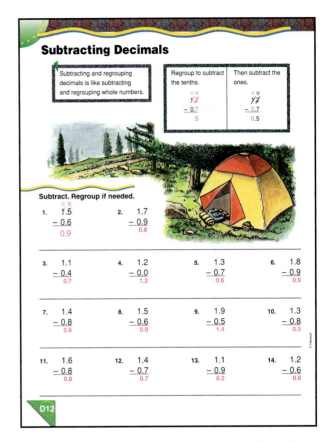

Teach Page D11 Define the vocabulary words for p. D11. Then, direct students' attention to the example exercise. Review the concept of subtracting like fractions. Solve Exercise 1 with the class. **How could you use fractions to write Exercise 1?** $\frac{4}{10} - \frac{1}{10} = \frac{3}{10}$

Guided Practice Have students solve Exercise 2. Check students' answers. **How could you use a comparison model to subtract tenths?** Line up models for each decimal. Compare the models to find the difference.

Independent Practice Assign Exercises 3–10. Note that none of the exercises require regrouping.

- You may wish to also teach p. D12 before students work independently.

Teach Page D12 Use decimal models, such as those found on p. D29, to demonstrate the example exercise and Exercise 1. Remind students that 1 whole can be regrouped as 10 tenths. **When do you need to regroup 1 whole as 10 tenths?** when there are not enough tenths to subtract

Guided Practice Have students solve Exercise 2. Check students' answers. **Why is it important to line up the decimal points?** so you subtract like place-values

Independent Practice Assign Exercises 3–14. Note that Exercises 4 and 9 do not require regrouping.

- After students complete p. D12, continue instruction to teach p. D13.

Book D T103

2 Teach and Practice continued

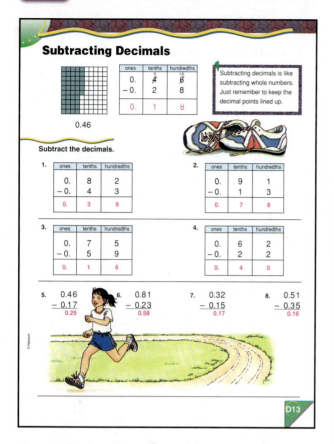

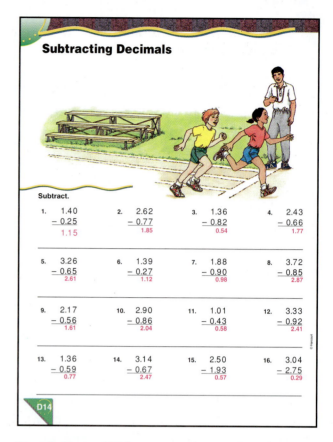

Teach Page D13 Discuss the example exercise. Have students cross out 0.28 of the shaded part. **Why is it helpful to use a place-value chart when subtracting decimals?** so you can keep place-values aligned correctly

Guided Practice Have students solve Exercise 1. Check students' answers. **How is subtracting decimals like subtracting whole numbers?** You line up like place-values and subtract from right to left, regrouping when necessary. **How is it different?** You subtract different place-values, and you include a decimal point.

Independent Practice Assign Exercises 2–8.

• You may wish to also teach p. D14 before students work independently.

Teach Page D14 Draw a place-value chart on the board to model Exercise 1. Discuss how to record regrouping. **Is regrouping needed in this problem? Explain.** Yes; you cannot subtract 5 hundredths from 0 hundredths, so one tenth will need to be regrouped as 10 hundredths.

Guided Practice Have students solve Exercise 2. Check students' answers. **How many times did you regroup when solving Exercise 2?** 2 times

Independent Practice Assign Exercises 3–16.

• After students complete p. D14, continue instruction to teach p. D15.

T104 First-Place Math

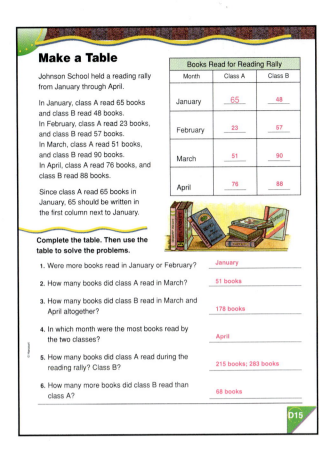

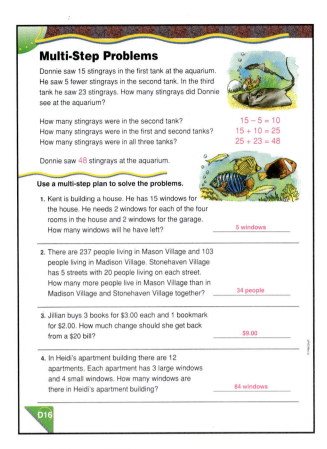

Teach Page D15 Use the data in the problem to complete the table for January and February. **In January and February were more books read by Class A or Class B? Explain.** Class B; $65 + 23 < 48 + 57$.

Guided Practice Have students complete the table and answer Problem 1. **What information is needed before you can solve the problem?** the total number of books that were read in January, $65 + 48 = 113$ and the total number of books that were read in February, $23 + 57 = 80$

Independent Practice Assign Problems 2–6.

- After students complete p. D15, continue instruction to teach p. D16.

Teach Page D16 Use 15 counters to show how many stingrays are in the first tank. Make an equivalent set, and remove 5 counters to show how many are in the second tank. Use 23 counters to show how many are in the third tank. **Can you multiply to find the total? Explain.** No; the groups are not equal, so you must add.

Guided Practice Have students solve Problem 1. Check students' answers. **What steps did you use to solve this problem?** Possible answer: multiplied to find the windows in the house: $2 \times 4 = 8$; added the windows in the garage: $8 + 2 = 10$; subtracted to find the number left: $15 - 10 = 5$ windows

Independent Practice Assign Problems 2–4.

- After students complete p. D16, continue instruction to teach p. D17.

Book D T105

3 Extra Practice

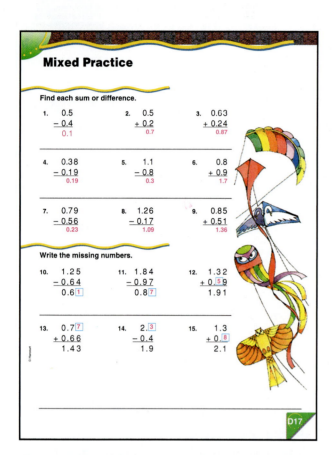

After students complete p. D17, you may wish to assign **Practice Activities**, p. P21.

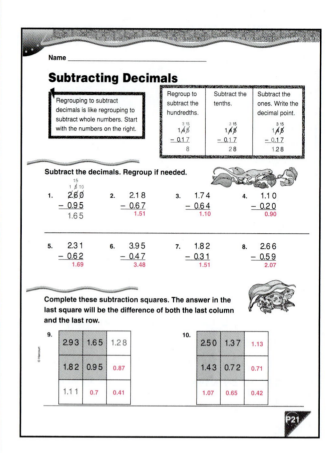

Teach Page D17 Direct students' attention to Exercises 10–15. Explain that they may want to try different strategies when trying to find the missing numbers. **How do you know whether to add or subtract in these exercises?** by looking at the operation sign

Guided Practice Have students solve Exercise 11. Check students' answers. **How did you find the missing number?** by regrouping 84 hundredths as 7 tenths 14 hundredths and then subtracting 7 hundredths from 14 hundredths to get 7 hundredths

Independent Practice Assign Exercises 1–10 and 12–15.

T106 First-Place Math

Teaching Notes

Week 4

Decimals
DAY 4
At a Glance

Objectives
- To add and subtract decimals

Problem Solving
- To solve problems using guess and check

1 Warm-Up Resources
- Number of the Day
- Problem of the Day
- Quick Review

Daily Warm-Up Flip Chart page 19

2 Teach and Practice
Book D • Decimals, pp. D18–D23

Manipulatives: Decimal models

3 Extra Practice
Practice Activities, p. P22

---

1 Warm-Up Resources

Have students work the following problems. Discuss their strategies and solutions.

Number of the Day
Write the value of a quarter as both a fraction of a dollar and a decimal. $\frac{1}{4}$, $0.25

Problem of the Day
Complete the magic square. The magic sum is 3.

1.6	0.2	1.2
0.6	1.0	1.4
0.8	1.8	0.4

Quick Review
Use <, >, or = to compare the decimals.

1. 47.5 ● 4.81 >
2. 3.2 ● 2.3 >
3. 2.8 ● 2.84 <
4. 9.9 ● 9.90 =

Vocabulary
- **decimal** — a number with one or more digits to the right of the decimal point (p. D18)
- **tenth** — one of ten equal parts (p. D18)
- **hundredth** — one of one hundred equal parts (p. D19)

T108 First-Place Math

2 Teach and Practice

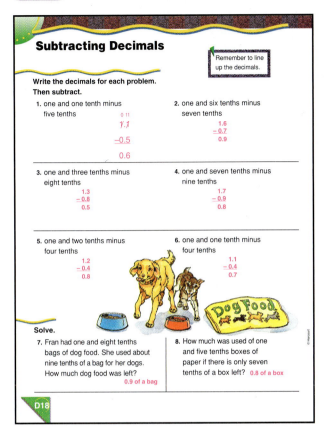

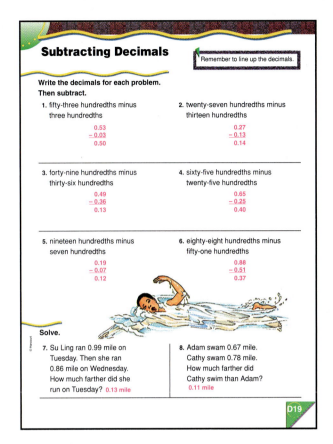

Teach Page D18 Define the vocabulary words for p. D18. Then, draw a place-value chart on the board to model Exercise 1. **When reading word names for decimals, why is the word *and* used?** It separates the whole number from the decimal part, so it tells where the decimal point is located.

Guided Practice Have students solve Exercise 2. Check students' answers. **How could decimal models be used to solve Exercise 2?** Start with one completely shaded decimal model and another model with 6 tenths shaded. Cross out the six tenths and one of the ten tenths. Nine tenths are left.

Independent Practice Assign Exercises 3–8.

- You may wish to also teach p. D19 before students work independently.

Teach Page D19 Define the vocabulary word for p. D19. Then, draw a place-value chart on the board to model Exercise 1. **Do you need to regroup to find the difference? Explain.** No; there are enough hundredths to subtract.

Guided Practice Have students solve Exercise 2. Check students' answers. **How could you use play money to model this problem?** Possible answer: Use 2 dimes and 7 pennies to show 0.27. Take away 1 dime and 3 pennies to subtract 0.13. You have 1 dime and 4 pennies, or 0.14, remaining.

Independent Practice Assign Exercises 3–8.

- After students complete p. D19, continue instruction to teach p. D20.

Book D T109

2 Teach and Practice continued

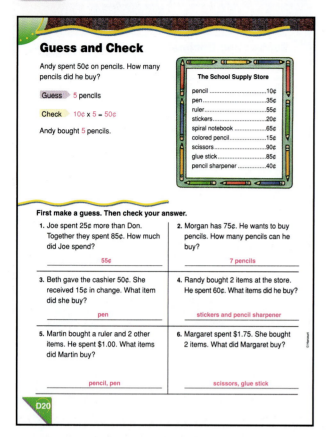

Teach Page D20 Discuss the example problem. Check the guess by multiplying to find the cost of 5 pencils. Since the total cost is 50¢, the guess is correct. Have students make a guess for Problem 1. **How can you check your guess?** Subtract 25¢ from your guess to find how much Don spent. Then add the two amounts to see how close the total is to 85¢.

Guided Practice Have students solve Problem 1. Check students' answers. **How did you change your guess to get the correct answer?** Possible answer: If the total is greater than 85¢, try a lesser amount. If the total is less than 85¢, try a greater amount.

Independent Practice Assign Problems 2–6.

- After students complete p. D20, continue instruction to teach p. D21.

Teach Page D21 Use decimal models, such as those found on p. D29, to demonstrate Exercises 1 and 10. For Exercise 10, ask, **Since 7 tenths + 2 tenths = 9 tenths, why isn't the missing number 9?** You need to also add the regrouped tenth.

Guided Practice Have students solve Exercise 11. Check students' answers. **Why is it helpful to record regrouping?** Showing how 24 hundredths were regrouped as 1 tenth 14 hundredths in the first step helps you find the missing number in the tenths column.

Independent Practice Assign Exercises 2–9 and 12–15.

- You may wish to also teach p. D22 before students work independently.

First-Place Math

Teach Page D22 Draw a picture to illustrate Exercise 1. **What operation will you use to solve the problem? Explain.** Addition; the question is asking for the total amount when two amounts are combined.

Guided Practice Have students solve Exercise 2. Check students' answers. **What operation will you use to solve the problem?** Since you want to find the total amount of flour, you add the amounts of white and wheat flour.

Independent Practice Assign Exercises 3–8.

• You may wish to also teach p. D23 before students work independently.

Teach Page D23 Use grid paper to model how to write Exercise 1. Explain how 10 tenths is regrouped as 1 whole 0 tenths. **How do you know whether the decimals are lined up correctly?** Make sure the decimal points are lined up and that the digits are in the correct place-value columns.

Guided Practice Have students solve Exercise 2. Check students' answers. **How could you use play money to model this problem?** Show 0.74 with 7 dimes and 4 pennies and show 0.19 with 1 dime and 9 pennies. 9 + 4 = 13 pennies or 1 dime and 3 pennies. 1 + 7 + 1 = 9 dimes. So, the total would be shown as 9 dimes and 3 pennies.

Independent Practice Assign Exercises 3–12.

Book D T111

3 Extra Practice

After students complete p. D23, you may wish to assign **Practice Activities,** p. P22.

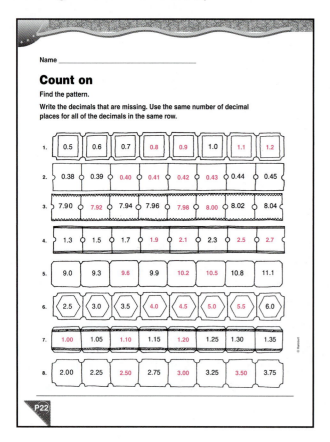

Teaching Notes

Teaching Notes

Week 4

Decimals

DAY 5 At a Glance

Objectives

- To add and subtract money
- To assess knowledge of decimals and problem solving

1 Warm-Up Resources

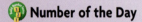Number of the Day
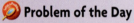Problem of the Day
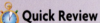Quick Review

page 20

2 Teach and Practice

Book D • Decimals, pp. D24–D26

Manipulatives:
 Decimals models
 Play money

3 Extra Practice

Practice Activities, pp. P23–P24
Game: Hoop Time

4 Wrap Up and Assess

Decimals Review, p. D27
Home Connection, p. D28
Book D Test, pp. 15–16

T114 First-Place Math

1 Warm-Up Resources

Have students work the following problems. Discuss their strategies and solutions.

Number of the Day

Find the number that is the value of 15 dollars, 3 quarters, two dimes, and one nickel. $16.00

Problem of the Day

Marta goes to the store to buy a sun visor that costs $12.50. She gives the cashier $20.00. Would Marta have enough change left over to buy a $5.00 bottle of sunscreen? Yes; her change from the sun visor would be $7.50, leaving her enough money to buy sunscreen.

Quick Review

1. 0.6 + 0.3 = ___ 0.9
2. 0.9 − 0.5 = ___ 0.4
3. 7.2 + 1.8 = ___ 9
4. 9.5 − 0.6 = ___ 8.9

Vocabulary

Review the vocabulary for Week 4.

decimal	a number with one or more digits to the right of the decimal point (p. D1)
decimal point	the mark in a decimal number that separates the ones and the tenths places (p. D4)
tenth	one of ten equal parts (p. D6)
hundredth	one of one hundred equal parts (p. D6)

2 Teach and Practice

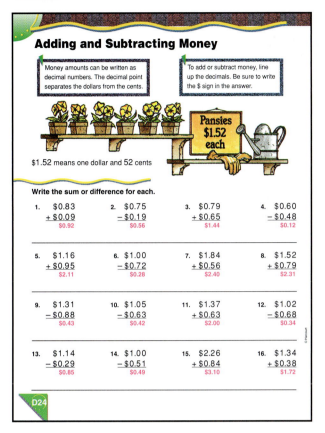

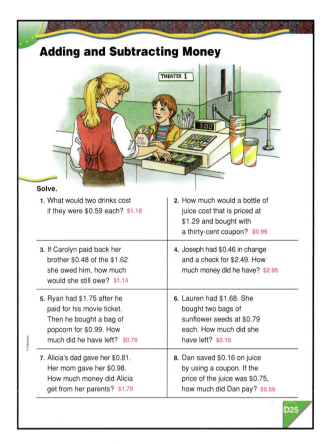

Teach Page D24 Use play money to represent $1.52. Discuss how decimals and money amounts are related. **What decimal part of a dollar does a penny show?** 0.01 **a dime?** 0.10 Use play money to model Exercise 1. Show how to regroup 12 pennies as 1 dime 2 pennies. Remind students to write the dollar sign in the answer.

Guided Practice Have students solve Exercise 2. Check students' answers. **How do you know whether to add or subtract?** by looking at the operation sign

Independent Practice Assign Exercises 3–16. Note that all of the exercises require regrouping in at least one place-value position.

• You may wish to also teach p. D25 before students work independently.

Teach Page D25 Use play money to model Exercise 1. Show two groups of 5 dimes 9 pennies. Record the addends on the board. **How do you record the sum of the pennies?** 9 + 9 = 18 pennies or 1 dime 8 pennies. Record a small 1 above the tenths column and record the 8 pennies in the hundredths column.

Guided Practice Have students solve Exercise 2. Check students' answers. **How did you know whether to add or subtract to solve this problem?** Since a coupon is used to decrease the cost of an item, you subtract the amount of the coupon from the price to find the new cost.

Independent Practice Assign Exercises 3–8.

• You may wish to also teach p. D26 before students work independently.

Book D T115

2 Teach and Practice continued

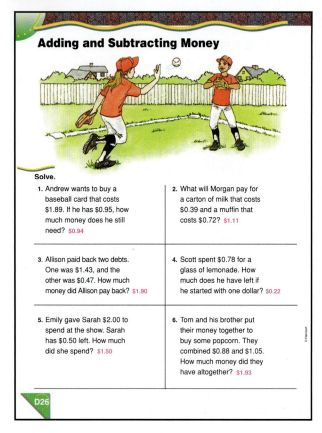

Teach Page D26 Use play money to model Exercise 1. Use a one dollar bill, 8 dimes, and 9 pennies to show the amount Andrew needs. Model how to take away $0.95 to find the amount he still needs. Regroup the dollar bill as 10 dimes. **What is another way to solve this problem?** Possible answer: Start with $0.95. Count up to the amount that Andrew needs.

Guided Practice Have students solve Exercise 2. Check students' answers. **Did you add or subtract to find the answer? Explain.** Add; the question is asking for the total cost of the items.

Independent Practice Assign Exercises 3–6.

Teaching Notes

T116 First-Place Math

3 Extra Practice

After students complete p. D26, you may wish to assign **Practice Activities,** pp. P23–P24.

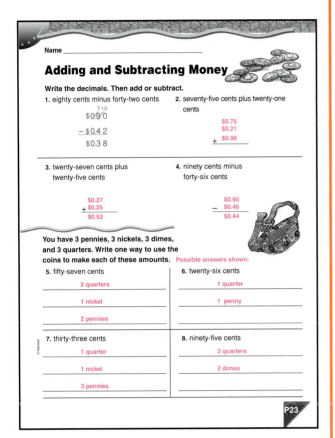

- You may also wish to have students play the game *Hoop Time* to practice decimal skills.

4 Wrap Up and Assess

Have students complete p. D27 to prepare for the Test.

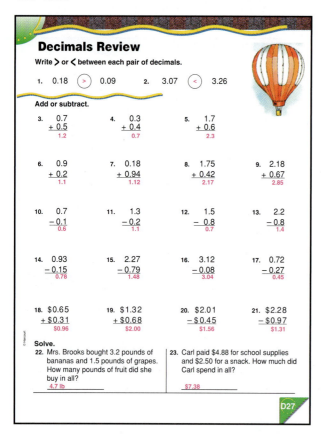

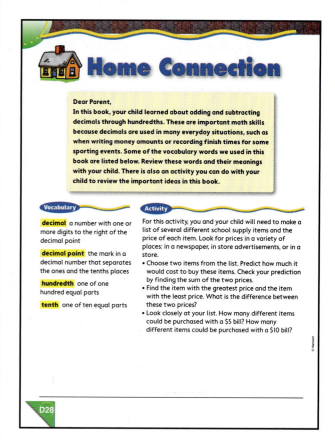

Use the following information to determine which pages students should review before taking the Book D Test.

Review Items	Skill	Review
1–2	Compare and Order Decimals	D1–D2
3–9	Add Decimals	D3–D8
10–17	Subtract Decimals	D11–D14
18–21	Add and Subtract Money	D24–D26
22–23	Solve Word Problems	D21–D23

Review the Home Connection page with students. You may want to preview the activity with students so they can explain it to their parents.

First-Place Math

Test

Have students complete the Test (**Assessment,** pp. 15–16) for Book D • Decimals.

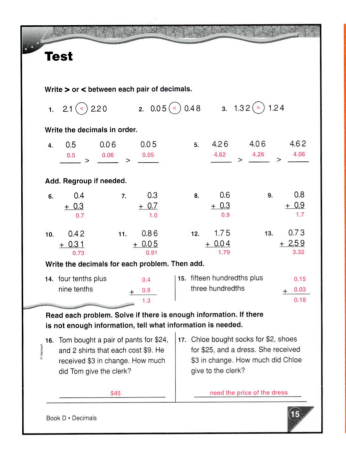

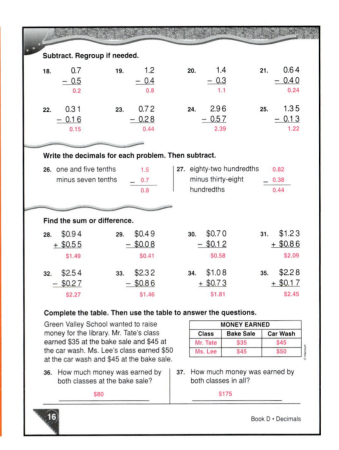

Test Items	Skill	Review
1–5	Compare and Order Decimals	D1–D2
6–15	Add Decimals	D3–D8
16–17	Too Little Information	D10
18–27	Subtract Decimals	D11–D14, D18–D19
28–35	Add and Subtract Money	D24–D26
36–37	Make a Table	D15

Check What Students Know

If a student answers an item incorrectly, refer to the "Review" column to determine where the related skill is taught. You may wish to record students' results on their record forms. (**Assessment,** p. 28)

Week 5 Planner

OBJECTIVES
SKILLS
- To identify plane and solid figures
- To identify and name points, lines, and segments
- To identify parallel lines and intersecting lines
- To identify and name rays and angles
- To identify right angles in plane figures
- To review multiplication and division
- To identify congruent figures and similar figures
- To identify lines of symmetry
- To identify and use ordered pairs

	DAY 1 pages T122–T125	**DAY 2** pages T126–T129
1 Warm-Up	**WARM-UP RESOURCES** Number of the Day, p. 21 Problem of the Day, p. 21 Quick Review, p. 21	**WARM-UP RESOURCES** Number of the Day, p. 22 Problem of the Day, p. 22 Quick Review, p. 22
2 Teach and Practice	Plane Figures, p. E1 Solid Figures, p. E2	Points, Lines, and Segments, p. E3 Parallel Lines and Intersecting Lines, p. E4 Rays and Angles, p. E5 Multi-Step Problems, p. E6
3 Extra Practice	Figure Faces, p. P25	Rays and Angles, p. P26
4 Wrap Up and Assess	**PRETEST** Book E Pretest, pp. 17–18 Assess knowledge of geometry and problem solving	

First-Place Math

Geometry

OBJECTIVES (CONTINUED)
PROBLEM SOLVING
- To solve problems using multiple steps
- To find a pattern
- To use logic to solve problems

DAY 3
pages T130–T133

WARM-UP RESOURCES
Number of the Day, p. 23
Problem of the Day, p. 23
Quick Review, p. 23

Right Angles, p. E7
Find a Pattern, p. E8
Mixed Review, pp. E9–E10

Right Angle Search, p. P27

DAY 4
pages T134–T139

WARM-UP RESOURCES
Number of the Day, p. 24
Problem of the Day, p. 24
Quick Review, p. 24

Congruent Figures, pp. E11–E12
Similar Figures, pp. E13–E14
Lines of Symmetry, p. E15
Use Logic, pp. E16–E17

Lines of Symmetry, p. P28

DAY 5
pages T140–T145

WARM-UP RESOURCES
Number of the Day, p. 25
Problem of the Day, p. 25
Quick Review, p. 25

Ordered Pairs, p. E18

Ordered Pairs, p. P29
Facts Practice, p. P30

Game: *Hoop Time*

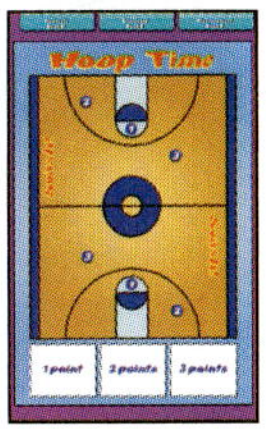

WRAP UP
Review, p. E19
Home Connection, p. E20

TEST
Book E Test, pp. 19–20
- Assess knowledge of geometry and problem solving

Book E T121

Week 5

Geometry

DAY 1 At a Glance

Objectives
- To identify plane and solid figures
- To assess knowledge of geometry and problem solving

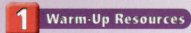
- Number of the Day
- Problem of the Day
- Quick Review

Book E Pretest, pp. 17–18

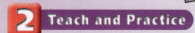

Book E • Geometry, pp. E1–E2

Manipulatives: Geometric solids

Practice Activities, p. P25

---

1 Warm-Up Resources

Have students work the following problems. Discuss their strategies and solutions.

Number of the Day
Using the number of sides of a triangle, write and solve one division problem and one multiplication problem using this number.
Possible answer: 36 ÷ 3 = 12; 12 × 3 = 36

Problem of the Day
How many triangles are shown? **16 triangles**

Quick Review
Name each figure.

1. **rectangle**
2. **cube**
3. **cylinder**
4. **triangle**

Vocabulary

hexagon	a polygon with 6 sides and 6 angles (p. E1)
octagon	a polygon with 8 sides and 8 angles (p. E1)
plane figure	a closed figure that lies in one plane (p. E1)
pentagon	a polygon with 5 sides and 5 angles (p. E1)
cylinder	a solid with 2 bases that are parallel circles (p. E2)
rectangular prism	a solid with 2 bases that are parallel rectangles (p. E2)
solid figure	a figure that lies in more than one plane (p. E2)

T122 First-Place Math

Pretest

Have students complete the Pretest (Assessment, pp. 17–18) for Book E • Geometry.

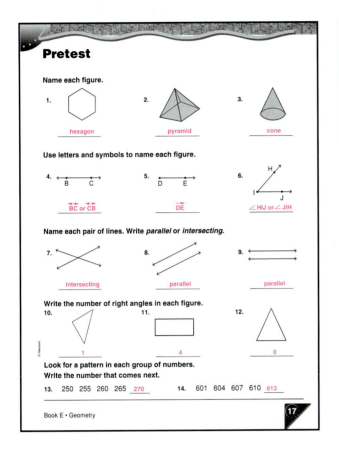
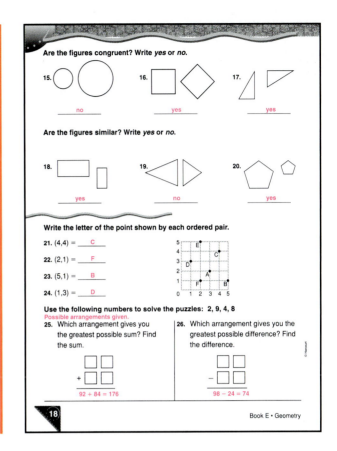

Pretest Items	Skill	Review
1	Plane Figures	E1
2–3	Solid Figures	E2
4	Points, Lines, and Segments	E3
5–6	Rays and Angles	E5
7–9	Parallel Lines and Intersecting Lines	E4
10–12	Right Angles	E7
13–14	Find a Pattern	E8
15–17	Congruent Figures	E11–E12
18–20	Similar Figures	E13–E14
21–24	Ordered Pairs	E18
25–26	Use Logic	E16–E17

Check What Students Know

If a student answers an item incorrectly, refer to the "Review" column to determine where the related skill is taught. You may wish to record students' results on their record forms. **(Assessment, p. 29)**

2 Teach and Practice

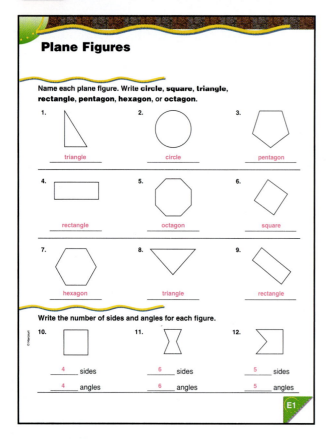

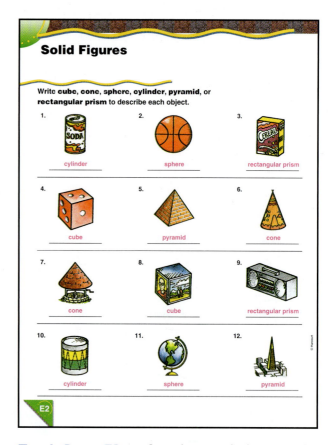

Teach Page E1 Define the vocabulary words for p. E1. Then, review the names and characteristics of plane figures. Identify and name the figure in Exercise 1. **How many sides does a triangle have?** 3 **How many angles?** 3

Guided Practice Have students complete Exercises 2 and 10. Check students' answers. **Can any square be called a rectangle?** Yes; since a rectangle is a 4-sided figure with 4 right angles, any square can be called a rectangle. **Can any rectangle be called a square? Explain.** No; since a square must have 4 equal sides, some rectangles are not squares.

Independent Practice Assign Exercises 3–9 and 11–12.

• After students complete p. E1, continue instruction to teach p. E2.

Teach Page E2 Define the vocabulary words for p. E2. Then, display the geometric solids. Review the names and characteristics of solid figures. Identify and name the figure in Exercise 1. **Does a cylinder have vertices? Explain.** No; a cylinder does not have any corners.

Guided Practice Have students complete Exercise 2. Check students' answers. **Does a sphere have faces, edges, and vertices? Explain.** No; a sphere has no flat surfaces or corners.

Independent Practice Assign Exercises 3–12.

T124 First-Place Math

3 Extra Practice

After students complete p. E2, you may wish to assign **Practice Activities,** p. P25.

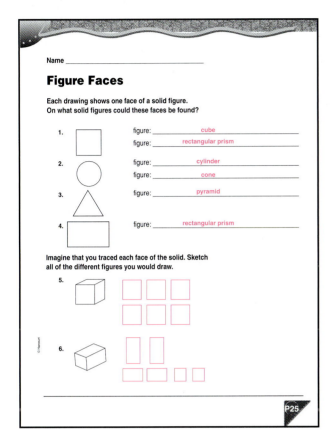

Book E T125

Week 5

Geometry

DAY 2 At a Glance

Objectives

- To identify and name points, lines, and segments
- To identify parallel lines and intersecting lines
- To identify and name rays and angles

Problem Solving

- To solve problems using multiple steps

1 Warm-Up Resources

- Number of the Day

- Problem of the Day
- Quick Review

2 Teach and Practice

Book E • Geometry, pp. E3–E6

Manipulatives: Play money

3 Extra Practice

Practice Activities, p. P26

---

1 Warm-Up Resources

Have students work the following problems. Discuss their strategies and solutions.

Number of the Day

Find the sum of the numbers of today's date and use them to write a multiplication problem.
Possible answer: Today is 6/20/02;
6 + 20 + 2 = 28; 28 × 5 = 140

Problem of the Day

Look at the figures below. What do they have in common?

  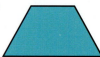

They each have 4 sides and 4 angles; they are all quadrilaterals.

Quick Review

Use <, >, or = to compare the number of sides that each figure has in the given pairs.

1. square ⊚ triangle
2. hexagon ⊚ octagon
3. pentagon ⊚ hexagon
4. rectangle ⊚ square

Vocabulary

point	a location on an object or in space (p. E3)
line segment	a part of a line that has two endpoints (p. E3)
parallel lines	lines that never intersect (p. E4)
intersecting lines	lines that cross each other at exactly one point (p. E4)
ray	a part of a line that begins at one endpoint and extends forever in one direction (p. E5)
right angle	an angle that forms a square corner and has a measure of 90° (p. E5)

First-Place Math

2 Teach and Practice

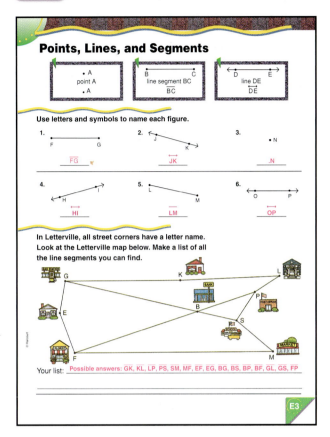

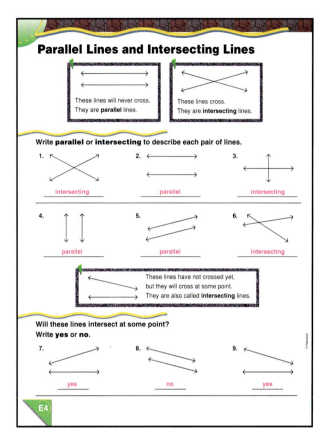

Teach Page E3 Define the vocabulary words for p. E3. Then, discuss the characteristics of each example. Tell students that the example line segment $\overline{BC}$ could also be named $\overline{CB}$, and that the example line $\overleftrightarrow{DE}$ could also be named $\overleftrightarrow{ED}$. Name the figure in Exercise 1 using letters and symbols. **What is the difference between a line and a line segment?** A line continues on; a line segment has 2 endpoints.

Guided Practice Have students complete Exercise 2. Check students' answers. Direct students' attention to the Letterville exercise. **How can you list the line segments in an organized way?** Possible answer: Start with one endpoint, and list each possible line segment that extends from it. Then repeat with each additional endpoint.

Independent Practice Assign Exercises 3–6 and the Letterville exercise.

- You may also wish to teach p. E4 before students work independently.

Teach Page E4 Define the vocabulary words for p. E4. Then, have students look for examples of each in the classroom. **Will parallel lines ever form angles? Explain.** No; parallel lines never cross to form angles.

Guided Practice Have students complete Exercises 1 and 7. Check students' answers. After they complete Exercise 7, ask, **How do you know that the lines will intersect?** Possible answer: You can extend each line to see that they cross.

Independent Practice Assign Exercises 2–6 and 8–9.

- After students complete p. E4, continue instruction to teach p. E5.

Book E T127

2 Teach and Practice continued

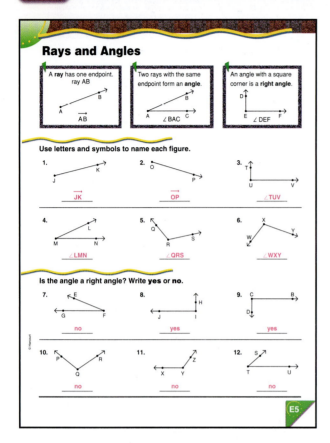

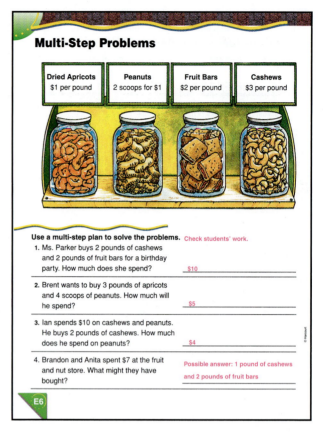

Teach Page E5 Define the vocabulary words for p. E5. Then, describe the characteristics of each example. Explain how each figure is named using letters and symbols. Tell students that angles are named by three letters, using the vertex as the middle letter. So, in the example, angle BAC could also be named angle CAB. **What is the difference between a ray and a line?** A ray has one endpoint; a line has no endpoints.

Guided Practice Have students complete Exercises 1 and 7. Check students' answers. **How can you check to see whether an angle is a right angle?** line up the corner of a sheet of paper with the angle

Independent Practice Assign Exercises 2–6 and 8–12.

Teach Page E6 Use play money to model Problem 1. Show 2 groups of $3 and 2 groups of $2. Multiply and then add to solve the problem. **What is another way to solve this problem?** Possible answer: Add the price for each pound of what Ms. Parker bought to find the total: $3 + $3 + $2 + $2 = $10

Guided Practice Have students solve Problem 2. Check students' answers. **What steps did you use to solve this problem?** Possible answer: I multiplied $1 by 3 to find the cost of the apricots and multiplied $1 by 2 to find the cost of the peanuts. Then I added to find the total. $3 + $2 = $5

Independent Practice Assign Problems 3–4. Have students share answers to Problem 4.

● After students complete p. E5, continue instruction to teach p. E6.

T128 First-Place Math

3 Extra Practice

After students complete p. E6, you may wish to assign **Practice Activities,** p. P26.

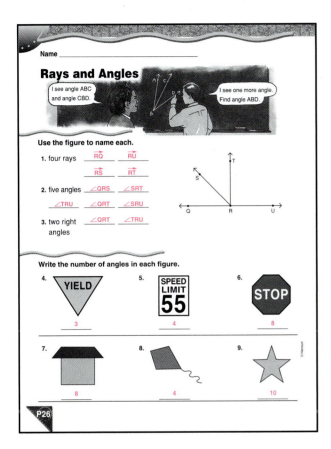

Teaching Notes

Book E T129

Week 5

Geometry

DAY 3 At a Glance

Objectives

- To identify right angles in plane figures
- To review multiplication and division

Problem Solving

- To find a pattern

1 Warm-Up Resources

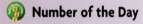 Number of the Day
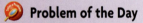 Problem of the Day
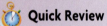 Quick Review

Daily Warm-Up Flip Chart page 23

2 Teach and Practice

Book E • Geometry, pp. E7–E10

3 Extra Practice

Practice Activities, p. P27

T130 First-Place Math

---

1 Warm-Up Resources

Have students work the following problems. Discuss their strategies and solutions.

Number of the Day

Use the number of years in 10 centuries to write one addition, one subtraction, one multiplication, and one division sentence. **Possible answer: 500 + 500 = 1,000; 2,000 − 1,000 = 1,000; 10 × 100 = 1,000; 1,000 ÷ 1 = 1,000**

Problem of the Day

Sam and Tina each have the same amount of money. Juan has $3 more than Sam. If they add all of their money together, the total amount would be $13.50. How much money does each person have? **Sam: $3.50, Tina: $3.50, Juan $6.50**

Quick Review

1. 305 ÷ 5 = **61**
2. 80 × 7 = **560**
3. 608 ÷ 8 = **76**
4. 236 × 3 = **708**

Vocabulary

pattern   a set of numbers or figures that have a relationship (p. E8)

2 Teach and Practice

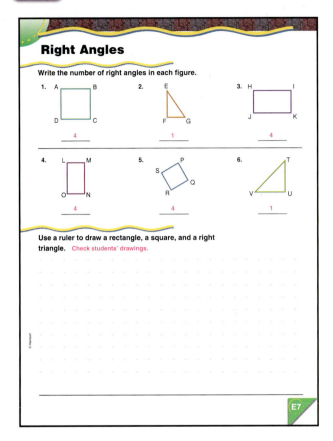

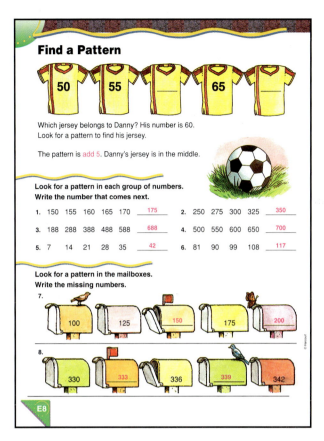

Teach Page E7 Use the corner of a sheet of paper to demonstrate how to test each angle in Exercise 1. **How can you use what you know about this figure to find the number of right angles?** Since all squares have 4 equal sides and 4 right angles, this figure has 4 right angles.

Guided Practice Have students complete Exercise 2. Check students' answers. **Using letters and symbols, how would you name the right angle of this triangle?** ∠EFG or ∠GFE

Independent Practice Assign Exercises 3–6, and have students complete the drawing activity.

• After students complete p. E7, continue instruction to teach p. E8.

Teach Page E8 Define the vocabulary word for p. E8. Then, have students describe the pattern in the jerseys and find the missing numbers. **What would be the number on a sixth jersey in this pattern?** 75

Guided Practice Have students solve Problem 1. Check students' answers. **How did you know the next number in the pattern?** Since the pattern is to add 5 to each number, the next number is 170 + 5, or 175.

Independent Practice Assign Problems 2–8. Note that all patterns can be described using addition. Some of the patterns can also be described as multiples of a number.

• After students complete p. E8, continue instruction to teach p. E9.

Book E   T131

2 Teach and Practice continued

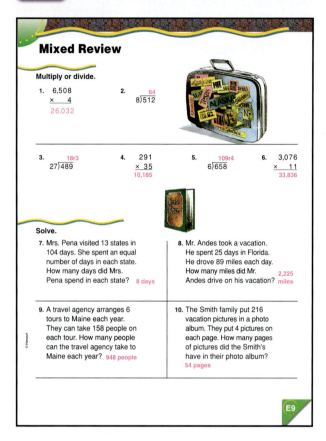

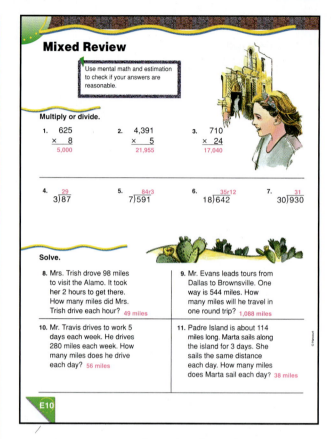

Teach Page E9 Write 6,508 × 4 vertically on the board. Talk through the steps, and remind students how to record regrouping. **How can you estimate to check whether your answer is reasonable?** Possible answer: Round the 4-digit factor to the nearest thousand. 7,000 × 4 = 28,000; since 26,032 is close to 28,000, the answer is reasonable.

Guided Practice Have students complete Exercise 2. Check students' answers. **How can you use estimation to decide where the first digit in the quotient is?** Possible answer: 480 ÷ 8 = 60. The first digit in the quotient will be in the tens place.

Independent Practice Assign Exercises 3–10.

● You may wish to also teach p. E10 before students work independently.

Teach Page E10 Show students how to solve Exercises 1 and 4. Review how to record regrouping when multiplying and how to record the steps in the division process. **How can you use mental math to check whether your answer to Exercise 4 is reasonable?** Possible answer: 90 ÷ 3 = 30. Since 29 is close to 30, the answer is reasonable.

Guided Practice Have students solve Exercise 2. Check students' answers. **How can you use estimation to check your answer to Exercise 2?** Possible answer: 5 × 4,000 = 20,000. Since 21,955 is close to 20,000, the answer is reasonable.

Independent Practice Assign Exercises 3 and 5–11.

T132 First-Place Math

3 Extra Practice

After students complete p. E10, you may wish to assign **Practice Activities**, p. P27.

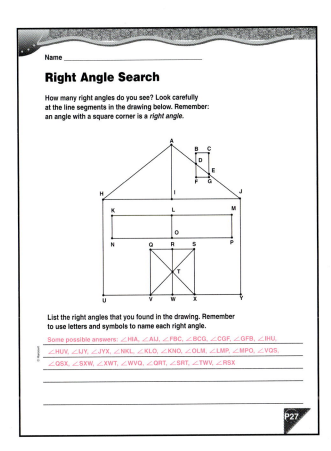

Teaching Notes

Week 5

Geometry

DAY 4 At a Glance

Objectives

- To identify congruent figures and similar figures
- To identify lines of symmetry

Problem Solving

- To use logic to solve problems

1 Warm-Up Resources

- Number of the Day
- Problem of the Day
- Quick Review

Daily Warm-Up Flip Chart page 24

2 Teach and Practice

Book E • Geometry, pp. E11–E17

Manipulatives: Pattern blocks

3 Extra Practice

Practice Activities, p. P28

---

1 Warm-Up Resources

Have students work the following problems. Discuss their strategies and solutions.

Number of the Day

Write three division sentences in which the dividend is the number of years in 1 century.
Possible answers: 100 ÷ 10 = 10; 100 ÷ 4 = 25; 100 ÷ 20 = 5

Problem of the Day

Look at the pattern. Draw the figure that would be next.

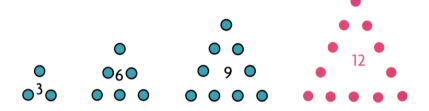

Quick Review

Multiply each number by 500.

1. 5 **2,500**
2. 20 **10,000**
3. 30 **15,000**
4. 90 **45,000**

Vocabulary

congruent figures	figures that have the same size and shape (p. E11)
similar figures	figures that have the same shape but might not have the same size (p. E13)
line of symmetry	a line that divides a figure into two congruent parts (p. E15)

T134 First-Place Math

2 Teach and Practice

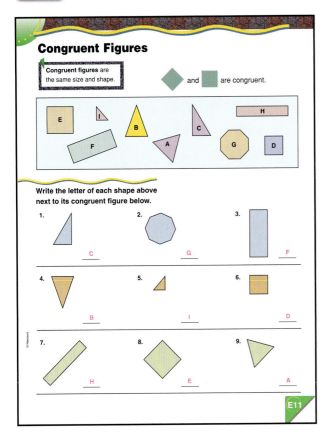

Teach Page E11 Define the vocabulary word for p. E11. Then, have students trace and cut out the squares in the example and compare them. **Do congruent figures always need to be in the same position? Explain.** No; congruent figures must be the same size and same shape, but they can be in any position.

Guided Practice Have students complete Exercise 1. Check students' answers. **Why isn't Figure I congruent to the figure in Exercise 1?** Although both are triangles, the two differ in shape and size.

Independent Practice Assign Exercises 2–9.

• You may wish to also teach p. E12 before students work independently.

Teach Page E12 Discuss the characteristics of the figures at the top of the page. **How are the first two figures similar?** They are both the same shape. **How are they different?** They are different sizes. You may wish to have students design their own pair of congruent figures and cut them out, using the grid paper found on p. E21.

Guided Practice Have students answer Exercise 1. Check students' responses. **What congruent figures do you see in the classroom?** Possible answers: windows, identical math books, desktops

Independent Practice Assign Exercises 2–5, and have students complete the drawing activity.

• After students complete p. E12, continue instruction on p. E13.

2 Teach and Practice continued

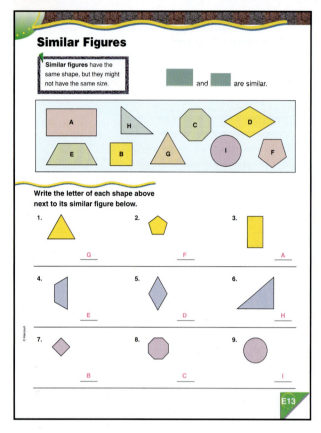

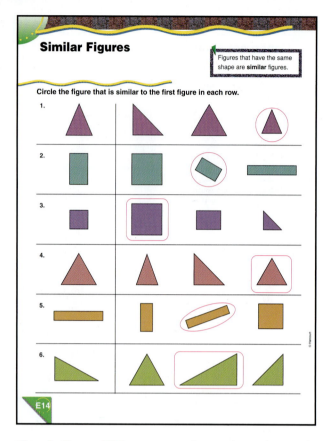

Teach Page E13 Define the vocabulary word for p. E13. Then, have students compare the rectangles at the top of the page. **Are all rectangles the same? Explain.** No; rectangles do not all have the same shape.

Guided Practice Have students find the figure that is similar to the figure in Exercise 1. Check students' answers. **Are all congruent figures also similar? Explain.** Yes; since congruent figures must be the same shape, they are also similar. **Are all similar figures also congruent? Explain.** No; since similar figures do not have to be the same size, they are not always congruent.

Independent Practice Assign Exercises 2–9.

- You may wish to also teach p. E14 before students work independently.

Teach Page E14 Have students describe each triangle in Exercise 1. **How can describing the triangles in the second column help you decide which one is similar to the triangle in the first column?** Similar figures must be the same shape. The first of the three triangles has a right angle and the second of the three triangles has 3 equal sides, so they cannot be similar to the triangle in the first column.

Guided Practice Have students complete Exercise 2. Check students' answers. **How did you know which figure was similar to the figure in the first column?** The square and the slender rectangle are different shapes and therefore are not similar.

Independent Practice Assign Exercises 3–6.

- After students complete p. E14, continue instruction on p. E15.

T136 First-Place Math

For an introductory activity using pattern blocks, see *More Manipulative Activities,* p. T181.

Modeling the Math

Use pattern blocks to make a figure that has a line of symmetry. Then have students use pattern blocks to work similar problems.

1. Fold a sheet of paper in half. Then, unfold the paper. Use the fold line as your line of symmetry to build a figure.

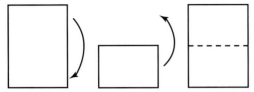

2. Using pattern blocks, start along the line of symmetry. Place a pattern block along your line of symmetry so that the pattern block is divided into 2 congruent parts.

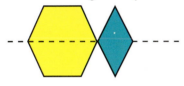

Or use two of the same pattern blocks at a time and place them so that each has the same side or point on the line of symmetry.

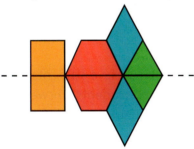

3. Then, continue to add pattern blocks until you have made a figure that you like.

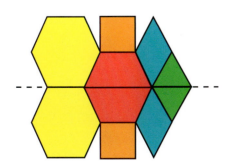

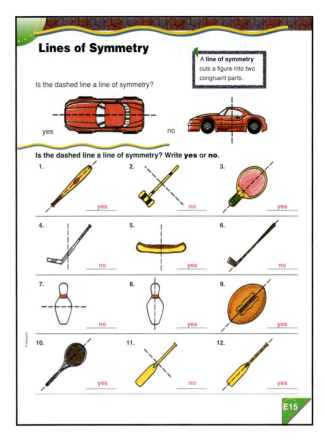

Teach Page E15 Define the vocabulary word for p. E15. Then, discuss the examples at the top of the page. **Why is the dashed line in the example on the right not called a line of symmetry?** because it does not divide the figure into two congruent parts Use pattern blocks to make a figure that would have a line of symmetry, as described in the *Modeling the Math.* Encourage students to use their blocks to make figures that would have lines of symmetry. Figures will vary.

Guided Practice Have students complete Exercise 1. Check students' answers. **Can a figure have more than one line of symmetry? Give an example.** Yes. Possible example: A rectangle has 2 lines of symmetry.

Independent Practice Assign Exercises 2–12.

● After students complete p. E15, continue instruction to teach p. E16.

Book E T137

2 Teach and Practice continued

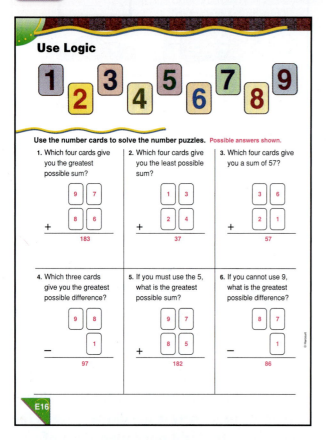

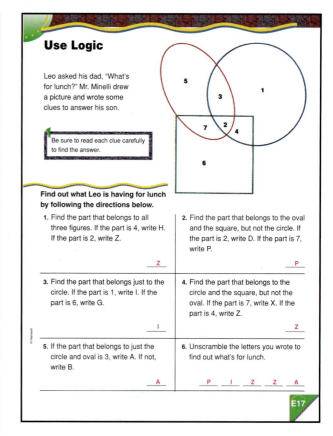

Teach Page E16 Use number cards to model Problem 1. Note that there are different arrangements possible. **Is it better to put the 8 and 9 in the ones place or the tens place? Explain.** Possible answer: Since you want greater numbers in positions with the greatest place-value, put the 8 and 9 in the tens place.

Guided Practice Have students complete Problem 2. Check students' answers. **What are two different ways to get the least possible sum?** 13 + 24 = 37 or 14 + 23 = 37

Independent Practice Assign Problems 3–6.

• You may wish to also teach p. E17 before students work independently.

Teach Page E17 Have students describe the three figures used in the Venn Diagram. Explain that the sections within the figures are each labeled with a number. **What does section 6 show?** the part that belongs just to the square

Guided Practice Have students solve Problem 1. Check students' answers. **How do you know which number belongs to all three figures?** The part with a 2 in it is the only part that is in the circle, the oval, and the square.

Independent Practice Assign Problems 2–6.

T138 First-Place Math

3 Extra Practice

After students complete p. E17, you may wish to assign **Practice Activities**, p. P28.

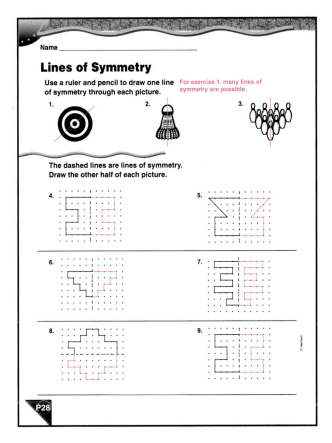

Teaching Notes

Book E T139

Week 5

Geometry

DAY 5 At a Glance

Objectives
- To identify and use ordered pairs
- To assess knowledge of geometry and problem solving

1 Warm-Up Resources
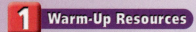
- Number of the Day
- Problem of the Day
- Quick Review

2 Teach and Practice
Book E • Geometry, p. E18

3 Extra Practice
Practice Activities, pp. P29–P30
Game: Hoop Time

Manipulatives:
Two-color counters

4 Wrap Up and Assess
Geometry Review, p. E19
Home Connection, p. E20
Book E Test, pp. 19–20

First-Place Math

---

1 Warm-Up Resources

Have students work the following problems. Discuss their strategies and solutions.

Number of the Day
Use the number of days in June to write three multiplication problems. **Possible answers:** $5 \times 6 = 30$, $30 \times 3 = 90$, $30 \times 10 = 300$

Problem of the Day
Write the next member of each group.
1. (0,0), (1,1), (2,2), (3,3) **(4,4)**
2. (0,0), (2,2), (4,4), (6,6) **(8,8)**
3. (0,0), (1,3), (2,6), (3,9) **(4,12)**
4. (0,2), (1,3), (2,4), (3,5) **(4,6)**

Quick Review
Find the value of the expression.
1. $30 \div x$ if $x = 6$ **5**
2. $7 \times y$ if $y = 3$ **21**
3. $a - 4$ if $a = 12$ **8**
4. $b \div 7$ if $b = 14$ **2**

Vocabulary
Review vocabulary for Week 5.

line segment	a part of a line that has two endpoints (p. E3)
intersecting lines	lines that cross each other at exactly one point (p. E4)
parallel lines	lines that never intersect (p. E4)
ray	a part of a line that begins at one endpoint and extends forever in one direction (p. E5)
right angle	an angle that forms a square corner and has a measure of 90° (p. E5)
line of symmetry	a line that divides a figure into two congruent parts (p. E15)
ordered pair	a pair of numbers used to locate a point on a grid (p. E18)

2 Teach and Practice

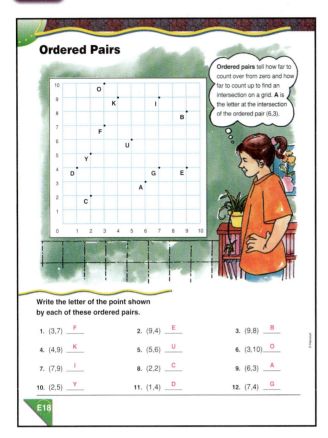

Teach Page E18 Define the vocabulary word for p. E18. Then, demonstrate how to locate point A on the grid. **Does the order of the numbers in an ordered pair make a difference? Explain.** Yes; the first number tells how many spaces to move right from the zero and the second number tells how many spaces to move up.

Guided Practice Have students complete Exercise 1. Check students' answers. **Can one number be used to name an intersection of lines on the grid? Explain.** No; you must have two numbers to tell where two lines cross.

Independent Practice Assign Exercises 2–12.

Teaching Notes

Book E T141

3 Extra Practice

After students complete p. E18, you may wish to assign **Practice Activities,** pp. P29–P30.

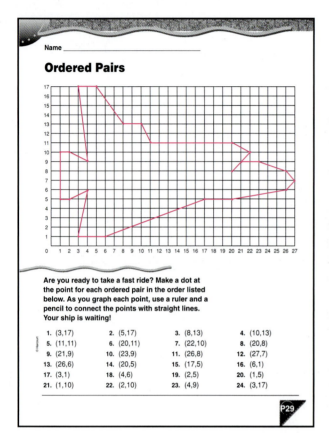

- You may also wish to have students play the game *Hoop Time* to practice geometry.

4 Wrap Up and Assess

Have students complete p. E19 to prepare for the Test.

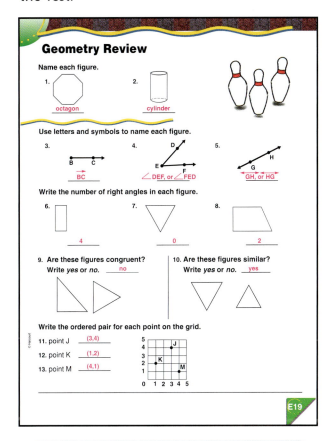

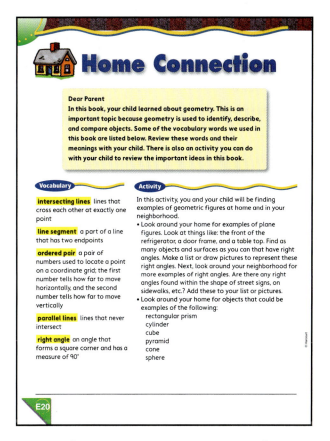

Review the Home Connection page with students. You may want to preview the activity with students so they can explain it to their parents.

Use the following information to determine which pages students should review before taking the Book E Test.

Pretest Items	Skill	Review
1	Plane Figures	E1
2	Solid Figures	E2
3–4	Rays and Angles	E5
5	Points, Lines, and Segments	E3
6–8	Right Angles	E7
9	Congruent Figures	E11–E12
10	Similar Figures	E13–E14
11–13	Ordered Pairs	E18

Book E T143

Test

Have students complete the Test (**Assessment**, pp. 19–20) for Book E • Geometry.

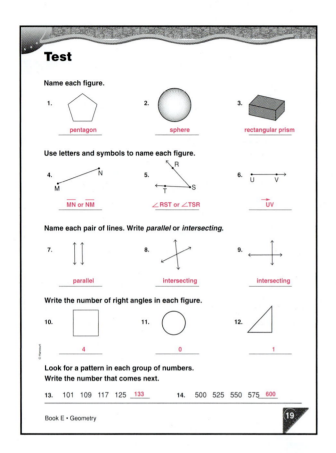

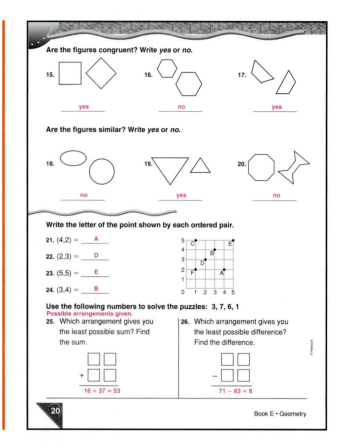

Test Items	Skill	Review
1	Plane Figures	E1
2–3	Solid Figures	E2
4	Points, Lines, and Segments	E3
5–6	Rays and Angles	E5
7–9	Parallel Lines and Intersecting Lines	E4
10–12	Right Angles	E7
13–14	Find a Pattern	E8
15–17	Congruent Figures	E11–E12
18–20	Similar Figures	E13–E14
21–24	Ordered Pairs	E18
25–26	Use Logic	E16–E17

Check What Students Know

If a student answers an item incorrectly, refer to the "Review" column to determine where the related skill is taught. You may wish to record students' results on their record forms.
(**Assessment**, p. 29)

First-Place Math

Teaching Notes

Week 6 Planner

OBJECTIVES

SKILLS
- To tell and estimate time
- To distinguish between A.M. and P.M.
- To find elapsed time
- To use a calendar
- To understand temperatures in Fahrenheit and in Celsius
- To measure objects to the nearest $\frac{1}{2}$ and $\frac{1}{4}$ inch
- To estimate length in customary and metric units
- To find the perimeter, area and volume of objects

	DAY 1 pages T148–T153	**DAY 2** pages T154–T159
1 Warm-Up	**WARM-UP RESOURCES** Number of the Day, p. 26 Problem of the Day, p. 26 Quick Review, p. 26	**WARM-UP RESOURCES** Number of the Day, p. 27 Problem of the Day, p. 27 Quick Review, p. 27
2 Teach and Practice	Telling Time, p. F1 Estimating Time, p. F2 A.M. and P.M., p. F3 Elapsed Time, p. F4 Calendar, p. F5 Degrees Fahrenheit, p. F6 Degrees Celsius, p. F7	Fractions of an Inch, p. F8 Estimating Feet, Yards, and Miles, pp. F9–F10 Measuring Millimeters and Centimeters, p. F11 Meters and Kilometers, p. F12 Multi-Step Problems, p. F13
3 Extra Practice	Telling Time, p. P31	Measuring Millimeters and Centimeters, p. P32
4 Wrap Up and Assess	**PRETEST** Book F Pretest, pp. 21–22 Assess knowledge of measurement and problem solving	

T146   First-Place Math

Measurement

OBJECTIVES (CONTINUED)

SKILLS (CONTINUED)
- To estimate capacity in customary and metric units
- To estimate weight in customary and metric units

PROBLEM SOLVING
- To solve problems using multiple steps
- To solve problems by making lists
- To solve problems using guess and check

DAY 3 pages T160–T163	DAY 4 pages T164–T169	DAY 5 pages T170–T175
WARM-UP RESOURCES Number of the Day, p. 28 Problem of the Day, p. 28 Quick Review, p. 28	**WARM-UP RESOURCES** Number of the Day, p. 29 Problem of the Day, p. 29 Quick Review, p. 29	**WARM-UP RESOURCES** Number of the Day, p. 30 Problem of the Day, p. 30 Quick Review, p. 30
Perimeter, p. F14 Area, pp. F15–F16 Make a List, p. F17	Cup, Pint, Quart, and Gallon, pp. F18–F19 Estimating Milliliters and Liters, pp. F20–F21 Volume, pp. F22–F23 Guess and Check, p. F24	Estimating Ounces, Pounds, and Tons, p. F25 Estimating Grams and Kilograms, p. F26
Area, p. P33	Perimeter, p. P34	Estimating Ounces, Pounds, and Tons, p. P35 Game: *Hoop Time*
		WRAP UP Review, p. F27 Home Connection, p. F28 **TEST** Book F Test, pp. 23–24 Assess knowledge of measurement and problem solving

Week 6
Measurement

DAY 1 At a Glance

Objectives

- To tell and estimate time
- To distinguish between A.M. and P.M.
- To find elapsed time
- To use a calendar to answer questions
- To understand temperatures in Fahrenheit and in Celsius
- To assess knowledge of measurement and problem solving

1 Warm-Up Resources

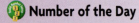
Number of the Day
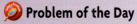
Problem of the Day
Quick Review

Book F Pretest, pp. 21–22

2 Teach and Practice

Book F • Measurement, pp. F1–F7

Manipulatives:
Two-color counters

3 Extra Practice

Practice Activities, p. P31

T148 First-Place Math

1 Warm-Up Resources

Have students work the following problems. Discuss their strategies and solutions.

Number of the Day

Multiply the number of hours in a day by the number of minutes in an hour to find the number of minutes in a day. **1,440 minutes**

Problem of the Day

The sum of the digits on a digital clock is 15. The number of minutes is 5 times as many as the number of hours. What time is shown on the clock? **7:35**

Quick Review

Name the time that is 15 minutes after each listed time.

1. 12:45 **1:00**
2. 4:30 **4:45**
3. 11:15 **11:30**
4. 10:45 **11:00**

Vocabulary

A.M.	the time between midnight and noon (p. F3)
P.M.	the time between noon and midnight (p. F3)
degrees Fahrenheit (°F)	a standard unit for measuring temperature in the customary system (p. F6)
degrees Celsius (°C)	a standard unit for measuring temperature in the metric system (p. F7)

Pretest

Have students complete the Pretest (Assessment, pp. 21–22) for Book F • Measurement.

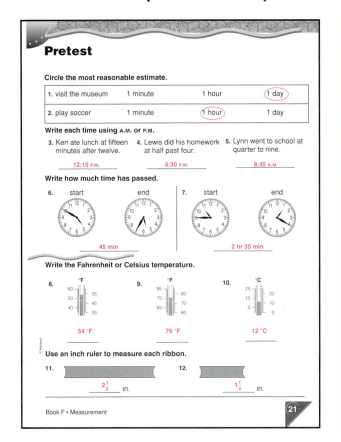
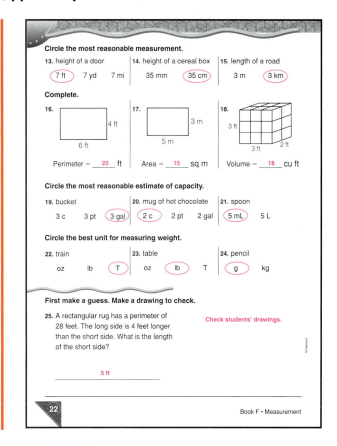

Pretest Items	Skill	Review
1–2	Estimate Time	F2
3–5	A.M. and P.M.	F3
6–7	Elapsed Time	F4
8–10	Degrees Fahrenheit/Celsius	F6–F7
11–12	Fractions of an Inch	F8
13	Estimate Feet, Yards and Miles	F9–F10
14	Measure Millimeters and Centimeters	F11
15	Meters and Kilometers	F12
16–18	Perimeter, Area and Volume	F14–F16, F22–F23
19–20	Cup, Pint, Quart, and Gallon	F18–F19
21	Estimate Milliliters and Liters	F20–F21
22–23	Estimate Ounces, Pounds, and Tons	F25
24	Estimate Grams and Kilograms	F26
25	Guess and Check	F24

Check What Students Know

If a student answers an item incorrectly, refer to the "Review" column to determine where the related skill is taught. You may wish to record students' results on their record forms. (**Assessment**, p. 30)

2 Teach and Practice

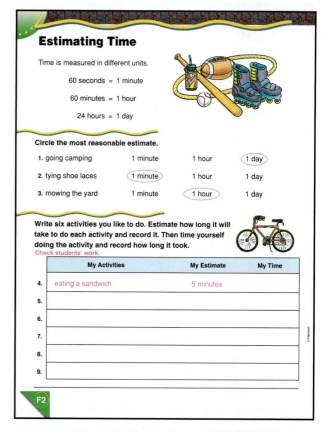

Teach Page F1 Review the meaning of *half* and *quarter*. **How many minutes are in an hour?** 60 min **a half hour?** 30 min **a quarter hour?** 15 min

Guided Practice Have students complete Exercises 1 and 5. Check students' answers. **What is another way to say the time given in Exercise 5?** Possible answers: quarter to eight or seven forty-five

Independent Practice Assign Exercises 2–4 and 6–10.

• After students complete p. F1, continue instruction to teach p. F2.

Teach Page F2 Display a clock with a second hand. Have students watch how the second hand moves for 1 minute. **What is the order, from least to greatest amount of time, of the terms *day, hour, minute,* and *second*?** second, minute, hour, day

Guided Practice Have students complete Exercise 3. Check students' answers. **Why is 1 hour the best choice?** Even if it takes a little less than an hour or a little more than an hour, 1 hour would still be the best estimate.

Independent Practice Assign Exercises 1–2. Have students complete Exercises 4–9 in class, if possible. You may wish to send the page home for students to complete.

• After students complete p. F2, continue instruction to teach p. F3.

T150 First-Place Math

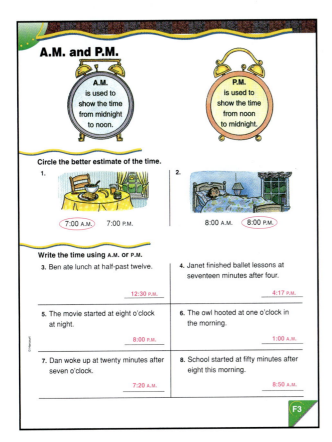

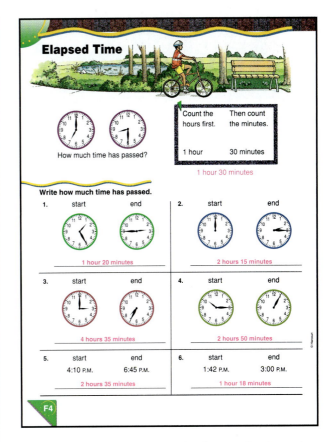

Teach Page F3 Define the vocabulary terms for p. F3. Then, draw a time line that shows a 24-hour day. Explain which hours are A.M. hours and which are P.M. hours. Discuss Exercise 1. **What clues are given in the picture that tell you it is 7:00 A.M.?** Possible answer: The sun is rising; the cereal and toast on the table are foods that are usually eaten at breakfast.

Guided Practice Have students complete Exercises 2 and 3. Check students' answers. **Why is the term "half-past" used to describe 30 minutes after the hour?** There are 60 minutes in an hour. Half of 60 is 30, so half of an hour or "half-past," is the same as 30 minutes after the hour.

Independent Practice Assign Exercises 4–8.

- After students complete p. F3, continue instruction to teach p. F4.

Teach Page F4 Draw 3 clocks on the board, showing 7:00, 8:00, and 8:30. **How much time has passed from 7:00 to 8:00?** 1 hr **How much time has passed from 8:00 to 8:30?** 30 min **How much time has passed in all from 7:00 to 8:30?** 1 hr 30 min Students may wish to use the clock faces found on p. F29 to do the exercises on finding elapsed time.

Guided Practice Have students solve Exercise 1. Check students' answers. **When the minute hand moves from one number to the next, how many minutes have passed?** 5 minutes

Independent Practice Assign Exercises 2–6.

- After students complete p. F4, continue instruction to teach p. F5.

2 Teach and Practice continued

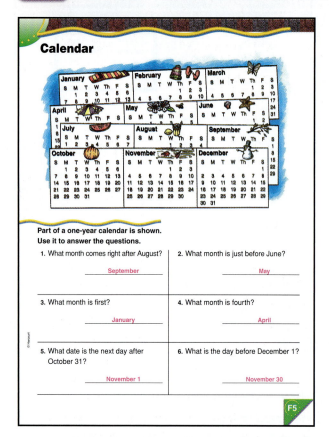

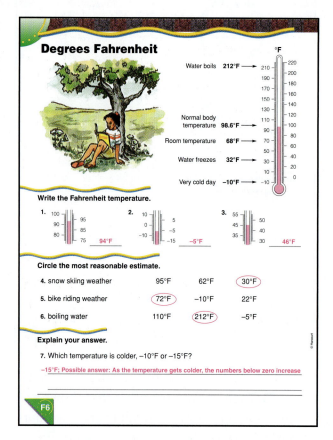

Teach Page F5 Display a 1-year calendar to review the order of the months. Discuss the number of days in each month. **What do the letters at the top of each calendar represent?** The days of the week: Sunday, Monday, Tuesday, Wednesday, Thursday, Friday, and Saturday

Guided Practice Have students answer Exercise 1. Check students' answers. **Do all months have the same number of days? Explain.** No; January, March, May, July, August, October, and December each have 31 days. February has either 28 or 29 days. The other months—April, June, September, and November—each have 30 days.

Independent Practice Assign Exercises 2–6.

- After students complete p. F5, continue instruction to teach p. F6.

Teach Page F6 Define the vocabulary word for p. F6. Then, discuss the temperatures given in the example. **Is it reasonable to say that the temperature of our classroom is 110°F? Explain.** No; normal room temperature is about 68°F.

Guided Practice Have students complete Exercises 1 and 4. Check students' answers. **How do you know that 95°F is not a reasonable estimate for snow skiing weather?** Since water freezes at 32°F, the snow would melt if the temperature was 95°F.

Independent Practice Assign Exercises 2–3 and 5–7. Have students share their responses to Exercise 7.

- You may wish to also teach p. F7 before students work independently.

T152 First-Place Math

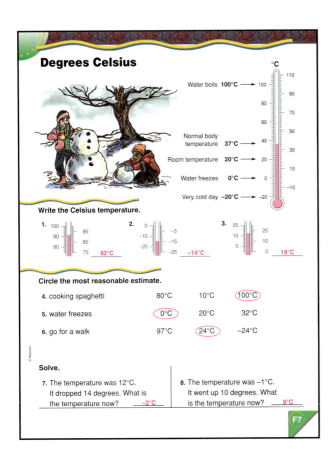

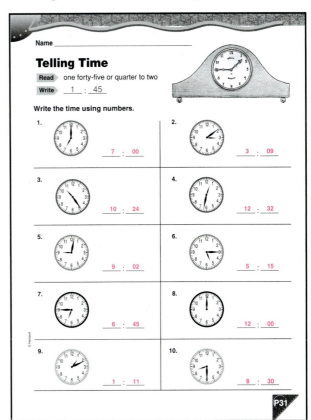

Teach Page F7 Define the vocabulary word for p. F7. Then, discuss the temperatures given in the example. **Is it reasonable to say that it could snow if the outside temperature is 0°C? Explain.** Yes, because water freezes at 0°C.

Guided Practice Have students complete Exercises 1 and 4. Check students' answers. **Are 100°F and 100°C close to the same temperature? Explain.** No; 212°F and 100°C are not close to the same temperature.

Independent Practice Assign Exercises 2–3 and 5–8.

After students complete p. F7, you may wish to assign **Practice Activities,** p. P31.

Book F T153

Week 6
Measurement

DAY 2 At a Glance

Objectives
- To measure objects to the nearest $\frac{1}{2}$ and $\frac{1}{4}$ inch.
- To estimate length in feet, yards, and miles
- To estimate length in metric units, such as millimeters, centimeters, meters, and kilometers

Problem Solving
- To solve problems using multiple steps

1 Warm-Up Resources

- Number of the Day
- Problem of the Day
- Quick Review

page 27

2 Teach and Practice

Book F • Measurement, pp. F8–F13

Manipulatives:
Two-color counters

3 Extra Practice

Practice Activities, p. P32

T154 First-Place Math

1 Warm-Up Resources

Have students work the following problems. Discuss their strategies and solutions.

Number of the Day
Take your age and multiply it by the number of days in a year. Add 1 day for each leap year since you were born. Add the number of days since your last birthday to find how many days old you are.
Answers will vary.

Problem of the Day
Chelsea, Jordan, and Tyler each have a different color and size of pencil. The red pencil is 6 in. long, and the blue one is 7 in. long. Chelsea's yellow pencil is 3 in. longer than Jordan's pencil. Tyler's pencil is 2 in. shorter than Chelsea's. How long is Chelsea's pencil? Who has the blue pencil?
9 in.; Tyler

Quick Review
Compare. Write >, <, or = for each ●.
1. $\frac{1}{2}$ ● $\frac{1}{4}$ >
2. $9\frac{2}{8}$ ● $9\frac{1}{4}$ =
3. $8\frac{5}{8}$ ● $8\frac{1}{4}$ >
4. $9\frac{1}{2}$ ● $9\frac{3}{4}$ <

Vocabulary

millimeter (mm)	a unit of length in the metric system (p. F11)
centimeter (cm)	a unit of length in the metric system; 1 centimeter = 10 millimeters (p. F11)
meter (m)	a unit of length in the metric system; 1 meter = 100 centimeters (p. F12)
kilometer (km)	a unit of length in the metric system; 1 kilometer = 1,000 meters (p. F12)

2 Teach and Practice

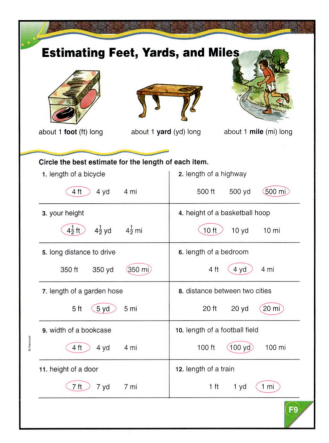

Teach Page F8 Review what each mark on the ruler shows. **How do you know that the rope measures $2\frac{1}{4}$ inches?** The end of the rope is lined up with the left end of the ruler. Each inch is divided into 4 equal parts. The marks show $\frac{1}{4}$ inches. The rope extends to the mark that is $\frac{1}{4}$ inch after the 2.

Guided Practice Have students measure the rope in Exercise 1. Check students' measurements. **Why is it helpful to measure items to the nearest fraction of an inch?** It provides a more accurate measurement of an object's actual length.

Independent Practice Assign Exercises 2–7.

- After students complete p. F8, continue instruction to teach p. F9.

Teach Page F9 Discuss the examples at the top of the page. **What is the difference between estimating the length and measuring the length of an object?** When you estimate, you tell about how long the object is; when you measure, you use a ruler or yardstick to determine the length.

Guided Practice Have students complete Exercise 1. Check students' answers. **How did you know the other estimates were not reasonable?** Possible answer: Four yards and four miles are units used to measure greater distances.

Independent Practice Assign Exercises 2–12.

- You may wish to also teach p. F10 before students work independently.

2 Teach and Practice continued

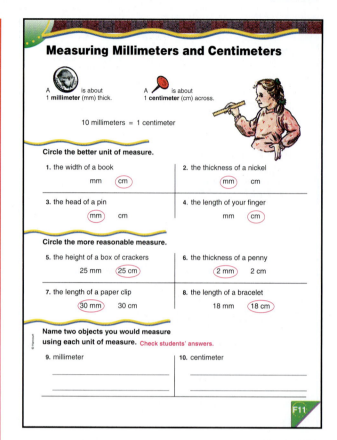

Teach Page F10 Discuss the examples at the top of the page. Display local maps to help students understand the length of a mile. **What is the order, from greatest to least length, of the terms *inch, foot, yard,* and *mile*?** mile, yard, foot, inch

Guided Practice Have students complete Exercises 1 and 5. Check students' answers. **For Exercise 1, how did you know which estimate was reasonable?** Possible answer: I used the picture of the 6 ft tall man as a reference. I estimated that a flagpole would be about twice as tall as a man.

Independent Practice Assign Exercises 2–4 and 6–10.

- After students complete p. F10, continue instruction to teach p. F11.

Teach Page F11 Define the vocabulary words for p. F11. Then, discuss the examples at the top of the page. **How can you use fractions to describe the relationship between 1 mm and 1 cm?** A millimeter is $\frac{1}{10}$ of a centimeter.

Guided Practice Have students complete Exercises 1 and 5. Check students' answers. **Why wouldn't the width of a book be measured in millimeters?** Possible answer: Millimeters are units used to measure very small things.

Independent Practice Assign Exercises 2–4 and 6–10.

- After students complete p. F11, continue instruction to teach p. F12.

T156 First-Place Math

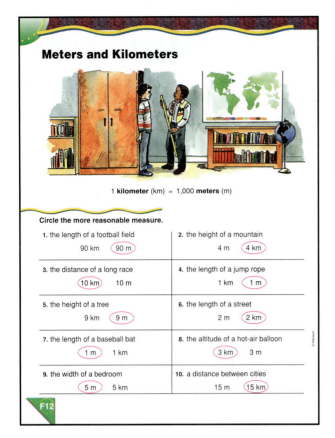

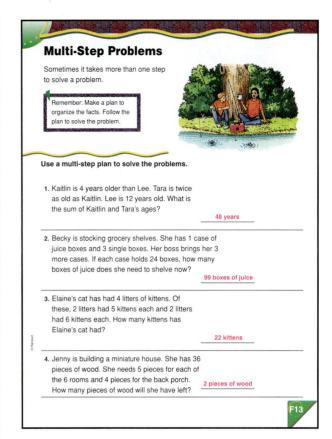

Teach Page F12 Define the vocabulary words for p. F12. Then, explain that a meter is about the length of a child's arm span and a kilometer is about the length of 10 football fields. **What is the order, from greatest to least length, of the terms *millimeter*, *centimeter*, *meter*, and *kilometer*?** kilometer, meter, centimeter, millimeter

Guided Practice Have students complete Exercise 1. Check students' answers. **What might you measure using kilometers?** Possible answers: the length of a street or the distance between two places

Independent Practice Assign Exercises 2–10.

• After students complete p. F12, continue instruction to teach p. F13.

Teach Page F13 Use counters to model Problem 1. Show 12 counters for Lee's age. For Kaitlin's age, make a set that is equivalent to Lee's and add 4 counters. For Tara's age, double the number of counters in Kaitlin's set. Add the sets for Kaitlin and Tara to solve the problem. **What operations did you use to solve this problem?** addition and multiplication

Guided Practice Have students solve Problem 2. Check students' work. **How many steps were used to solve this problem? Explain.** Possible answer: 3. Add 1 case and 3 cases to get 4 cases. Multiply 4 by 24 boxes to get 96 boxes. Add 96 boxes and 3 boxes to get 99 boxes.

Independent Practice Assign Problems 3–4.

3 Extra Practice

After students complete p. F13, you may wish to assign **Practice Activities**, p. P32.

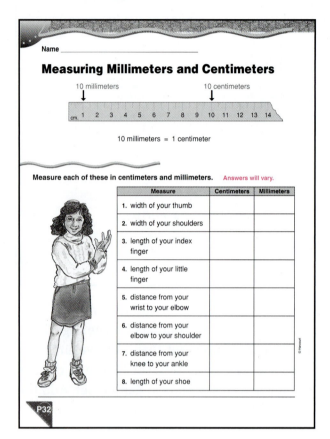

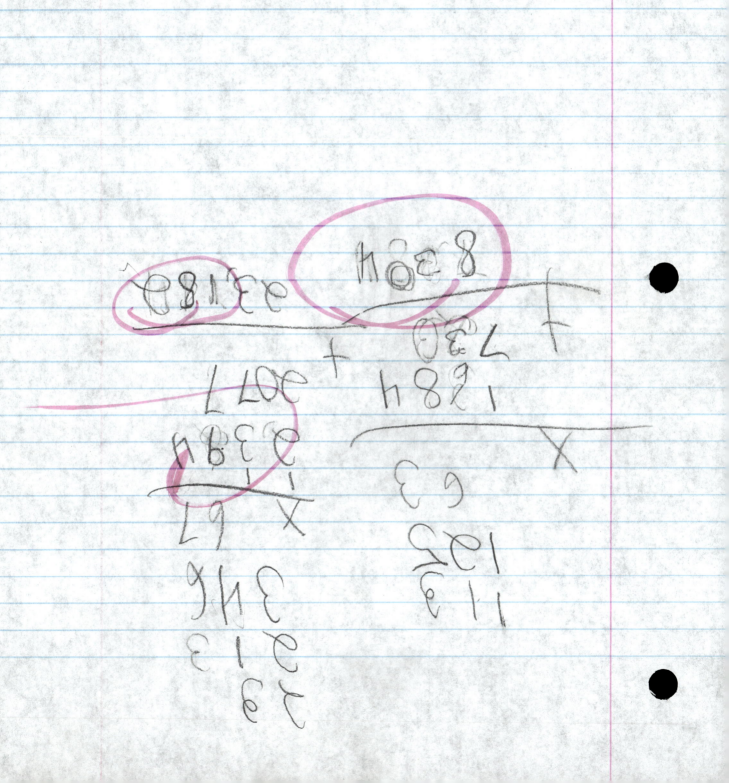

Teaching Notes

Week 6
Measurement

DAY 3 At a Glance

Objectives
- To find the perimeter and area of objects

Problem Solving
- To solve problems by making a list

1 Warm-Up Resources
- Number of the Day
- Problem of the Day
- Quick Review

Daily Warm-Up Flip Chart, page 28

2 Teach and Practice
Book F • Measurement, pp. F14–F17

Manipulatives:
Geoboards
Color tiles

3 Extra Practice
Practice Activities, p. P33

---

1 Warm-Up Resources

Have students work the following problems. Discuss their strategies and solutions.

Number of the Day
The number of the day is the number of sides that an octagon has. Write all the factors of this number. 1, 2, 4, 8

Problem of the Day
Arrange these figures in the order described below. Write the name of each figure in the new order.

The first figure has six sides. The third figure has one less side than the first figure. The fifth figure has three sides. The octagon is between the hexagon and the pentagon. The quadrilateral is before the triangle. hexagon, octagon, pentagon, quadrilateral, triangle

Quick Review
Compare. Write >, <, or = for each ●.

1. $3 \times 4 \bullet 8 + 3$ >
2. $34 \bullet 9 \times 4$ <
3. $9 \times 2 \bullet 29 - 11$ =
4. $25 + 19 \bullet 7 \times 7$ <

Vocabulary
perimeter — the distance around a figure (p. F14)

area — the number of square units needed to cover a given surface (p. F15)

First-Place Math

2 Teach and Practice

For an introductory activity using geoboards, see *More Manipulative Activities,* p. T182.

Modeling the Math

Use geoboards to find the perimeter of a 3 × 4 rectangle. Then have students use geoboards to work similar problems.

1. Show a rectangle that is 4 units long and 3 units wide.

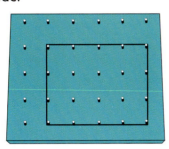

Count units along the four sides of the rectangle to find the perimeter.

4 + 3 + 4 + 3 = 14

So, the perimeter is 14 units.

2. Show a rectangle that is 5 units wide and has a perimeter of 18 units.

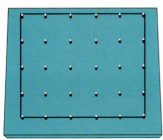

What is the length of the rectangle?
4 units

3. Show a figure that is not a rectangle and has a perimeter of 18 units.

Possible answer:

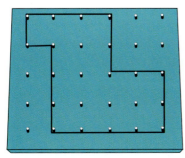

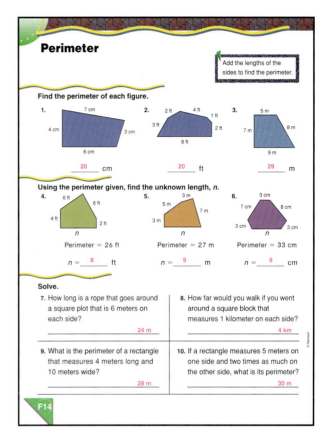

Teach Page F14 Define the vocabulary word for p. F14. Then, use geoboards to review how to find the perimeter of a rectangle, as described in the *Modeling the Math.* Direct students' attention to Exercise 1. **What number sentence could you write to find the perimeter of this figure?** 7 + 3 + 6 + 4 = 20 Remind students that the perimeter is "20 cm," not "20." Ask students to make a figure on a geoboard with a perimeter of 10 units. Check students' work.

Guided Practice Have students complete Exercise 4. Check students' answers. **How can you find the missing length?** Add to find the total of the known sides. 4 + 6 + 6 + 2 = 18 ft. Subtract that from the given perimeter to find the missing length. 26 − 18 = 8 ft.

Independent Practice Assign Exercises 2–3 and 5–10.

- After students complete p. F14, continue instruction to teach p. F15.

Book F T161

2 Teach and Practice continued

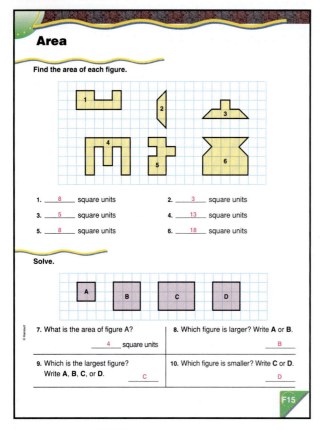

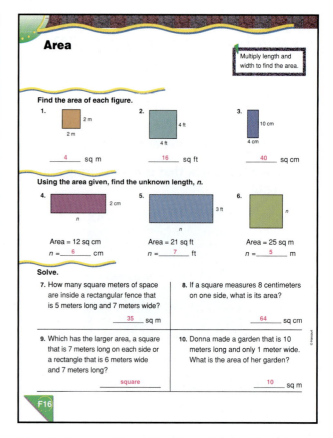

Teach Page F15 Define the vocabulary word for p. F15. Then, use grid paper to model finding the area of Figure 1. Suggest marking or shading squares as you count so that squares are not added twice. **What is the area of 1 square on the grid?** 1 square unit

Guided Practice Have students find the area of Figure 2. **What is the total area of the 2 triangles in the figure?** 1 square unit **Explain how you know.** Each triangle is half of one square. $\frac{1}{2} + \frac{1}{2} = 1$.

Independent Practice Assign Exercises 3–10.

• You may wish to also teach p. F16 before students work independently.

Teach Page F16 Use color tiles to model Exercise 1. Show 2 rows of 2 squares. Explain that when the figure is on a grid, you can count squares or use multiplication to find the area. **For Exercise 1 what multiplication sentence can you use to find the area?** $2 \times 2 = 4$ Students may wish to use the grid paper found on p. F29 to do the exercises.

Guided Practice Have students complete Exercise 4. Check students' answers. **How did you find the unknown length?** Possible answer: Think: $n \times 2 = 12$; since $6 \times 2 = 12$, $n = 6$ cm.

Independent Practice Assign Exercises 2–3 and 5–10.

• After students complete p. F16, continue instruction to teach p. F17.

T162 First-Place Math

3 Extra Practice

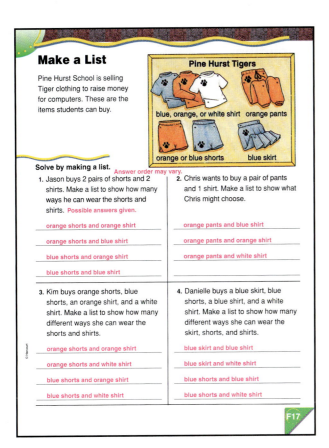

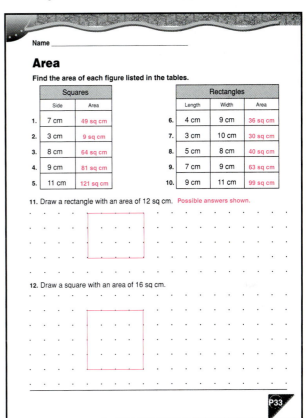

After students complete p. F17, you may wish to assign **Practice Activities**, p. P33.

Teach Page F17 Draw a diagram to illustrate Problem 1. **How can you make an organized list to record all of the combinations?**
Possible answer: Start with one pair of shorts, and list it with each shirt. Then list the other pair of shorts with each shirt.

Guided Practice Have students solve Problem 2. Check students' answers. **Is there more than one possible list for this problem? Explain.** No; there is only one choice for the pants, and the list shows all possible combinations with these pants and each shirt.

Independent Practice Assign Problems 3–4. Note that the order of combinations may vary.

Book F T163

Week 6
Measurement

DAY 4 At a Glance

Objectives
- To choose the best unit for measuring capacity using cup, pint, quart, and gallon
- To estimate capacity in milliliters and liters
- To find the volume of objects

Problem Solving
- To solve problems using guess and check

1 Warm-Up Resources
- Number of the Day
- Problem of the Day
- Quick Review

Daily Warm-Up Flip Chart page 29

2 Teach and Practice
Book F • Measurement, pp. F18–F24

Manipulatives: Connecting cubes

3 Extra Practice
Practice Activities, p. P34

---

1 Warm-Up Resources

Have students work the following problems. Discuss their strategies and solutions.

Number of the Day
Write the number of weeks in a year as a product of prime factors. $2 \times 2 \times 13 = 52$

Problem of the Day
A number has the digits 0, 3, and 6. Two of the digits are used twice. Is this number the number of seconds in a day or the number of inches in a mile? What is the number?
the number of inches in a mile; 63,360

Quick Review
Multiply each number by 4.
1. 8 **32**
2. 12 **48**
3. 7 **28**
4. 22 **88**

Vocabulary

cup (c)	a customary unit used to measure capacity (p. F18)
pint (p)	a customary unit used to measure capacity; 1 pint = 2 cups (p. F18)
quart (qt)	a customary unit for measuring capacity; 1 quart = 2 pints (p. F18)
gallon (gal)	a customary unit used to measure capacity; 1 gallon = 4 quarts (p. F18)
liter (L)	a unit of capacity in the metric system; 1 liter = 1,000 milliliters (p. F20)
volume	the measure of the space a solid figure occupies (p. F22)

T164 First-Place Math

2 Teach and Practice

Teach Page F18 Define the vocabulary words for p. F18. Then, discuss the examples at the top of the page. **What is the order, from greatest to least capacity, of the terms *cup*, *pint*, *quart*, and *gallon*?** gallon, quart, pint, cup

Guided Practice Have students complete Exercise 1. Check students' answers. **How do you choose the best unit for measuring the capacity of an object?** Possible answer: Although any unit can be used, it is best to find the largest unit that makes sense.

Independent Practice Assign Exercises 2–10.

• You may wish to also teach p. F19 before students work independently.

Teach Page F19 Review the units of capacity: cup, pint, quart, and gallon. **What are some items you would measure using each unit?** Possible answers: cup of rice, pint of cream, quart of juice, gallon of milk

Guided Practice Have students complete Exercise 1. Check students' answers. **Since there are 2 pints in a quart, what is a reasonable estimate of the pot's capacity in pints?** 8 pints

Independent Practice Assign Exercises 2–8.

• After students complete p. F19, continue instruction to teach p. F20.

Book F T165

2 Teach and Practice continued

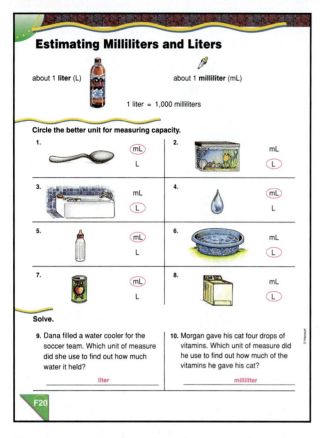

Teach Page F20 Define the vocabulary word for p. F20. Then, discuss the examples at the top of the page. **Which unit of measurement would be the better unit to measure the capacity of a pitcher?** liter

Guided Practice Have students complete Exercise 1. Check students' answers. **What are you measuring when you measure the capacity of a spoon?** the amount the spoon can hold

Independent Practice Assign Exercises 2–10.

- You may wish to also teach p. F21 before students work independently.

Teach Page F21 Discuss the examples at the top of the page. **How many milliliters are there in 1 liter?** 1,000

Guided Practice Have students complete Exercise 1. Check students' answers. Tell students that a glass of milk holds about 250 mL. **For Exercise 1 about how many glasses of milk are in the jug of milk?** about 8 glasses

Independent Practice Assign Exercises 2–10.

- After students complete p. F21, continue instruction to teach p. F22.

T166 First-Place Math

For an introductory activity using connecting cubes, see *More Manipulative Activities*, p. T183.

Modeling the Math

Use three colors of connecting cubes to find the volume of a 2 × 5 × 3 figure. Then have students use connecting cubes to work similar problems.

1. Use cubes to build a 2 × 5 × 1 figure.

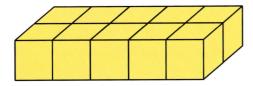

How many cubes did you use? 10 cubes

What is the volume of the figure? 10 cubic units

2. Use second color to build a second layer measuring 2 × 5 units on top of the first figure.
   What is the volume of the figure?

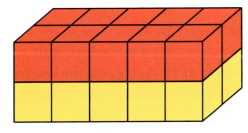

2 × 5 × 2 = 20 cubic units

3. Use a third color to build a third layer.
   What is the volume of the figure?

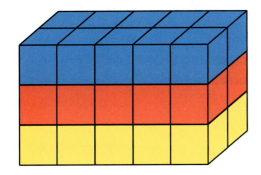

2 × 5 × 3 = 30 cubic units

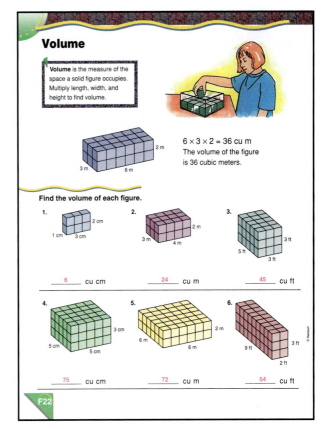

Teach Page F22 Define the vocabulary word for p. F22. Then, use connecting cubes to find the volume of a rectangular figure, as described in the *Modeling the Math*. Have students use connecting cubes to model the figure in the example exercise. Explain that the cubes can be counted to find the volume. **Why can you multiply the dimensions of the figure to find the volume?** Possible answer: You are finding the total of a 3-dimensional array; 2 layers of 3 rows of 6 cubes = 2 × 3 × 6 = 36 cubic units.

Guided Practice Have students complete Exercise 1. Check students' answers. **What are two ways to find the volume of this figure?** Possible answer: Count the cubes; multiply the length, width, and height of the figure.

Independent Practice Assign Exercises 2–6.

- You may wish to also teach p. F23 before students work independently.

Book F

2 Teach and Practice continued

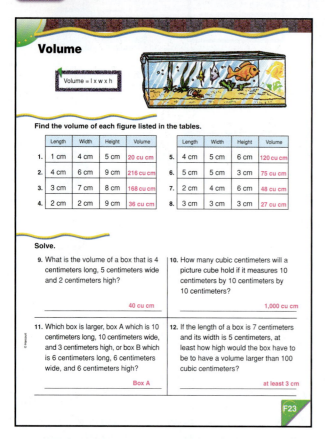

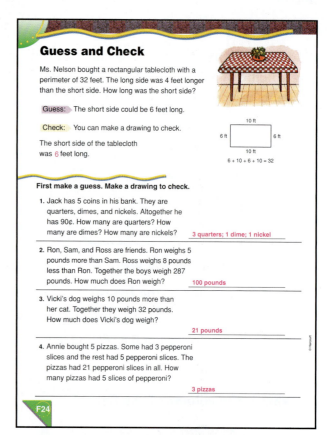

Teach Page F23 Use connecting cubes to model the dimensions given in Exercise 1. **What multiplication sentence can you use to find the volume of this figure?** $1 \times 4 \times 5 = 20$ cu cm

Guided Practice Have students complete Exercise 2. Check students' answers. **Why might you multiply to find the volume instead of count or add cubes?** Possible answers: If a figure is large, it might be simpler to multiply its dimensions; in a figure, it is sometimes hard to count "hidden" cubes.

Independent Practice Assign Exercises 3–12.

• After students complete p. F23, continue instruction to teach p. F24.

Teach Page F24 Read through the example with students. **For a tablecloth with a perimeter of 40 feet, guess the length of the short side.** Guesses should be greater than 6 ft. Have students make drawings to check their guesses. **What would the measurements of this tablecloth be?** The length of the short side would be 8 ft, and the length of the long side would be 12 ft.

Guided Practice Have students solve Problem 1. Check students' answers. **How did you change your guess to get closer to the correct answer?** Possible answer: by trying different combinations of coins until you got a combination that totaled 90¢

Independent Practice Assign Problems 2–4.

T168 First-Place Math

3 Extra Practice

After students complete p. F24, you may wish to assign **Practice Activities,** p. P34.

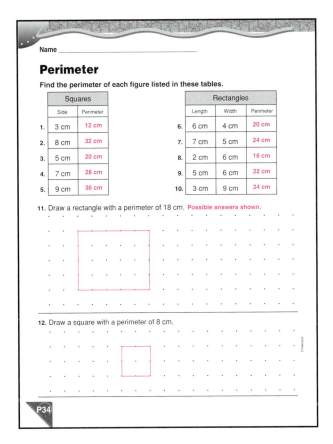

Teaching Notes

Book F T169

Week 6
Measurement

DAY 5 At a Glance

Objectives
- To estimate weight in customary units, including ounces, pounds, tons
- To estimate weight in metric units, including grams and kilograms
- To assess knowledge of measurement and problem solving

1 Warm-Up Resources
- Number of the Day
- Problem of the Day
- Quick Review

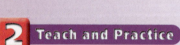

2 Teach and Practice
Book F • Measurement, pp. F25–F26

3 Extra Practice
Practice Activities, p. P35
Game: Hoop Time

Manipulatives:
  Two-color counters

4 Wrap Up and Assess
Measurement Review, p. F27
Home Connection, p. F28
Book F Test, pp. 23–24

T170 First-Place Math

1 Warm-Up Resources

Have students work the following problems. Discuss their strategies and solutions.

Number of the Day
Write the current month as a number, and list its first five multiples. **Possible answer: If the month is June, the number is 6 and the first 5 multiples would be 6, 12, 18, 24, 30.**

Problem of the Day
Jane says she has as many brothers as there are quarts in a half-gallon and as many sisters as there are cups in a half-pint. What is the total number of children in her family? **4 children**

Quick Review
Multiply each number by 16.

1. 8 **128**   2. 10 **160**   3. 11 **176**   4. 12 **192**

Vocabulary
Review vocabulary for Week 6.

meter (m)	a unit of length in the metric system; 1 m = 100 cm (p. F12)
perimeter	the distance around a figure (p. F14)
area	the number of square units needed to cover a given surface (p. F15)
quart (qt)	a customary unit for measuring capacity; 1 qt = 2 pt (p. F18)
liter (L)	a unit of capacity in the metric system; 1 L = 1,000 mL (p. F20)
volume	the measure of the space a solid figure occupies (p. F22)
ounce (oz)	a customary unit used for measuring weight; 16 oz = 1 lb (p. F25)
gram (g)	a unit of mass in the metric system; 1,000 grams = 1 kilogram (p. F26)

2 Teach and Practice

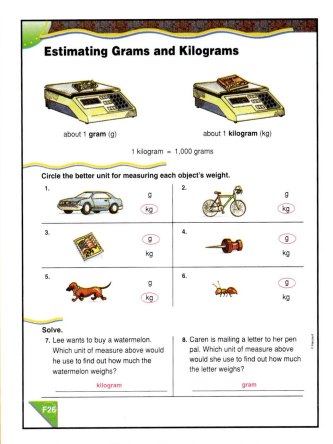

Teach Page F25 Define the vocabulary word for p. F25. Then, discuss the examples at the top of the page. **What is the order, from least weight to greatest weight, of the terms *pound*, *ounce*, and *ton*?** ounce, pound, ton

Guided Practice Have students complete Exercise 1. Check students' answers. **Can two objects have the same weight but be different sizes? Give an example.** Yes; a paper clip and a sheet of paper are different sizes but weigh about the same.

Independent Practice Assign Exercises 2–12.

● After students complete p. F25, continue instruction to teach p. F26.

Teach Page F26 Define the vocabulary word for p. F26. Then, discuss the examples at the top of the page. Explain that grams and kilograms are metric units. **What are you measuring when you measure the mass of an object?** the weight of an object

Guided Practice Have students complete Exercise 1. Check students' answers. **If there are 1,000 grams in 1 kilogram, how many grams are there in 4 kilograms?** 4,000 grams

Independent Practice Assign Exercises 2–8.

Book F T171

3 Extra Practice

After students complete p. F26, you may wish to assign **Practice Activities**, p. P35.

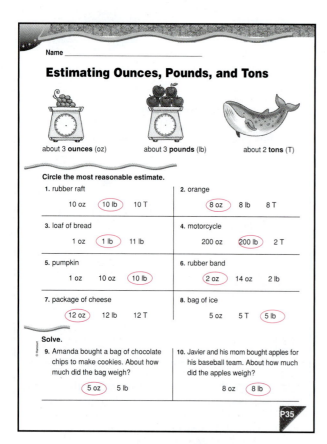

- You may also wish to have students play the game *Hoop Time* to practice measurement.

Teaching Notes

T172 First-Place Math

4 Wrap Up and Assess

Have students complete p. F27 to prepare for the Test.

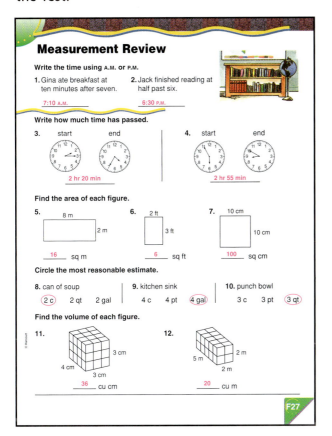

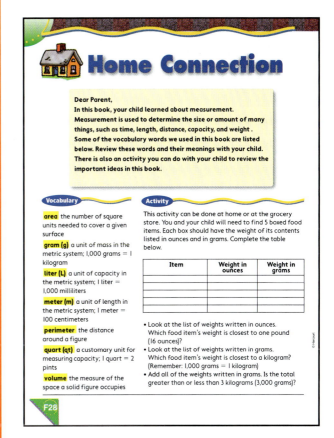

Use the following information to determine which pages students should review before taking the Book F Test.

Review Items	Skill	Review
1–2	A.M. and P.M.	F3
3–4	Elapsed Time	F4
5–7	Area	F15–F16
8–10	Cup, Pint, Quart, and Gallon	F18–F19
11–12	Volume	F22–F23

Review the Home Connection page with students. You may want to preview the activity with students so they can explain it to their parents.

Book F

Test

Have students complete the Test (**Assessment**, pp. 23–24) for Book F • Measurement.

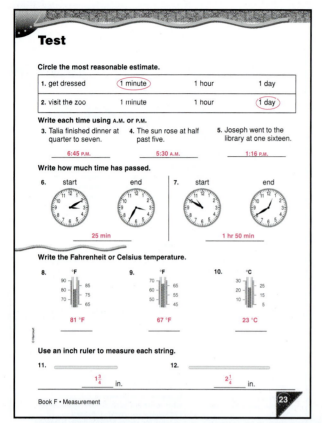
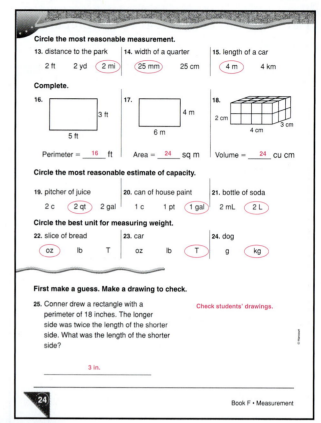

Test Items	Skill	Review
1–2	Estimate Time	F2
3–5	A.M. and P.M.	F3
6–7	Elapsed Time	F4
8–10	Degrees Fahrenheit/Celsius	F6–F7
11–12	Fractions of an Inch	F8
13	Estimate Feet, Yards and Miles	F9–F10
14	Measure Millimeters and Centimeters	F11
15	Meters and Kilometers	F12
16–18	Perimeter, Area and Volume	F14–F16, F22–F23
19–20	Cup, Pint, Quart, and Gallon	F18–F19
21	Estimate Milliliters and Liters	F20–F21
22–23	Estimate Ounces, Pounds, and Tons	F25
24	Estimate Grams and Kilograms	F26
25	Guess and Check	F24

Check What Students Know

If a student answers an item incorrectly, refer to the "Review" column to determine where the related skill is taught. You may wish to record students' results on their record forms. (**Assessment**, p. 30)

Teaching Notes

More Manipulative Activities

Base-Ten Blocks

PARTNERS

Objective
- To use base-ten blocks to show models of numbers

Materials
- base-ten blocks, paper, and pencil

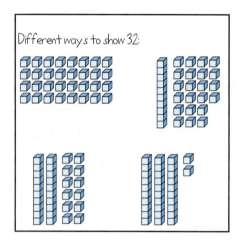

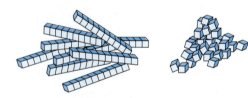

Show the Ways

Get Ready
- One player in each pair will need to record the pair's responses.
- Players will use base-ten blocks (ones and tens blocks) to show 32 in as many different ways as they can.

Let's Play
- Have partners use ones and tens blocks to show 48 in as many different ways as they can.
- Have the recorder sketch each base-ten model of the number.
- The pair with the most models for the number wins. Have students repeat these steps for the numbers 53, 115, and 122. (For 3-digit numbers, students can also use hundreds blocks in some of their models).

Other Ways to Play
- Have each pair use base-ten blocks to find as many different 3-digit numbers as possible using the digits 1, 4, and 6. Have the recorder list each number and make a sketch of the model. The pair with the most 3-digit numbers wins.
- **Challenge** Have pairs use base-ten blocks to show 243. The first pair that can model 243 using 18 blocks wins. Possible answer: 1 hundred, 14 tens, and 3 ones

Counters

PARTNERS

Objective
- To use counters to model multiplication and division situations

Materials
- 2 number cubes labeled 2–7, counters, 7 paper plates, paper, and pencil

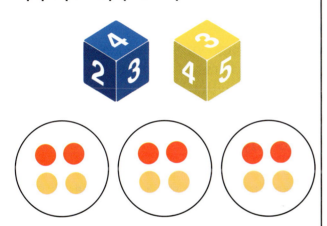

Counter Stories

Get Ready
- Have students practice modeling multiplication and division using counters. Ask students to model 4 × 3 by placing 3 counters on each of 4 plates. Ask students to model 12 ÷ 3 by showing 12 counters divided equally among 3 plates.
- Discuss how multiplication and division are related. Review fact families by having students write the four related multiplication and division sentences for 3, 5, and 15.

Let's Play
- Player A rolls the number cubes. One number is used to represent the number of groups, and the other represents the number in each group.
- Player A uses the counters and paper plates to model the equal groups. He or she records the multiplication sentence and then uses the sentence to tell a multiplication story.
- Player B records a related division sentence and then uses it to tell a division story.

Other Ways to Play
- Have each player write 4 addition, subtraction, multiplication, or division story problems. Partners trade problems and use counters to show how to solve the problems.
- **Challenge** Have students use the numbers rolled to make a 2-digit number. This 2-digit number is then used as the product or the dividend in the story. Note that this activity may require students to use multiplication and division skills beyond basic facts.

First-Place Math

Fraction Bars

PARTNERS

Objective
- To use fraction bars to explore comparing fractions to the benchmarks 1, 0, and $\frac{1}{2}$

Materials
- fraction bars, paper, and pencil

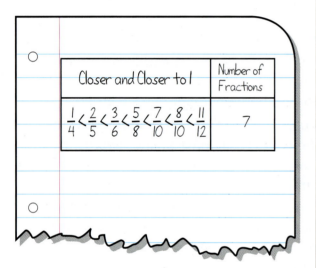

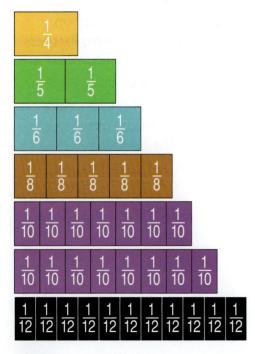

Closer and Closer

Get Ready
- Have each pair prepare a recording sheet. Pairs play against other pairs in the class.

Let's Play
- Player A chooses a fraction that can be modeled with fraction bars and records it. Encourage students to begin with a fraction that is as close to 0 as possible.
- Player B finds a fraction that is only slightly greater than Player A's fraction. He or she records the fraction on the recording sheet.
- Players take turns and continue until the pair cannot use fraction bars to find a fraction that is closer to 1. The pair with the most fractions listed wins.

Other Ways to Play
- Have pairs begin with 1 whole fraction bar. Players take turns choosing fractions that get closer to 0.
- **Challenge** Have pairs begin with $\frac{1}{12}$. Players take turns choosing fractions that get closer to $\frac{1}{2}$.

Fraction Circles

PARTNERS

Objective
- **To use fraction circles to explore identifying fractions**

Materials
- fraction circles, timer or stopwatch, paper, and pencil

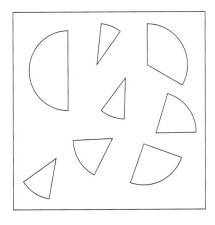

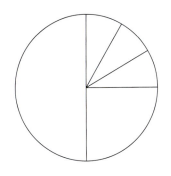

Fraction Time

Get Ready
- Have each player make a game board by tracing one of each different fraction circle piece on a sheet of paper ($\frac{1}{2}$, $\frac{1}{3}$, $\frac{1}{4}$, $\frac{1}{5}$, $\frac{1}{6}$, $\frac{1}{8}$, $\frac{1}{10}$, and $\frac{1}{12}$ pieces).
- Encourage students to mix up the pieces and trace them in different orientations. Their partner will need to identify each piece, so make sure that there are no labels on the game board.

Let's Play
- Partners trade game boards and place them face down. Set the timer for 30 seconds. Both players turn over their game boards and begin identifying each fraction circle piece.
- Once 30 seconds have passed, players use fraction circle pieces to check their work. The player to correctly identify the most pieces wins.

Other Ways to Play
- Have students make new game boards with any mix of 24 fraction circle pieces. Remind students that there will not be just one of each piece. Set the timer for 1 minute and play again.
- **Challenge** Have students make new game boards by tracing 4 whole circles on their game boards. Then have students find different fraction pieces to fill each circle and trace each piece. Set the timer for 2 minutes and play again.

First-Place Math

Decimal Models

PARTNERS

Objective
- To use decimal models to explore the relationship between fractions and decimals (tenths and hundredths)

Materials
- index cards, decimal models (tenths and hundredths), paper, and pencil

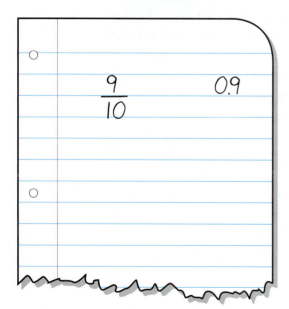

It's All Relative

Get Ready
- Have each pair write the following on 10 index cards: 1 tenth, 3 tenths, 4 tenths, 7 tenths, 9 tenths, 2 hundredths, 15 hundredths, 26 hundredths, 48 hundredths, 81 hundredths.

Let's Play
- Have each pair shuffle the cards and place them face down in a stack.
- Player A takes a card from the top of the stack. He or she shades an appropriate decimal model to show the amount and records the amount using a fraction and a decimal.
- Players take turns until all the cards are used. Players score 1 point for each correct model, fraction, and decimal.

Other Ways to Play
- Have players prepare 10 additional index cards. These cards should show the decimal form for the amounts written in word form on the original set of cards. Pairs shuffle all index cards and play a memory game in which they match the word form and the decimal form.
- **Challenge** Have each student begin with 2 hundredths models. The cards are shuffled and placed face down in a stack. The players take turns picking cards and shading the amounts on their decimal models. Each amount is added to the previous amount already shaded. After all the cards are used, the player with the greater amount shaded wins.

Pattern Blocks

PARTNERS

Objective
- To use pattern blocks to develop spatial sense

Materials
- pattern blocks, paper, and pencil

Pattern Block Puzzles

Get Ready
- Have each player fold a sheet of paper in half two times and open it up.
- Have each player use pattern blocks to make 4 different designs that fit in each of the areas on the paper.
- Have each player trace only the outline of each design. These figures are the pattern block puzzles that the opponent will use for the activity.

Let's Play
- Have partners trade puzzles. Each player uses pattern blocks to fill each design. He or she then records the solution by tracing the pattern blocks on the puzzle. Pattern block puzzles may be filled in different ways than originally designed.

Other Ways to Play
- When players design pattern block puzzles, have them record the number of pattern blocks used to make each design. Their partner must then fill the puzzle using the same number of blocks.
- **Challenge** Have players make and trace just one design on each paper leaving the other 3 areas of the paper blank. Partners trade puzzles and then attempt to find as many different ways to fill the same design as possible. Each way is recorded in a different area of the paper. The player with more combinations wins.

First-Place Math

Geoboards

PARTNERS

Objective
- **To use geoboards to explore perimeter**

Materials
- geoboards, rubber bands, dot paper, and pencil

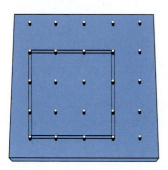

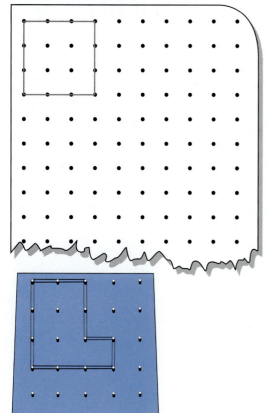

Perimeter Time

Get Ready
- Each player needs a geoboard, some rubber bands, a pencil, and dot paper.

Let's Play
- For Round 1, each player uses a geoboard to make as many different squares as possible. Each square must be recorded on dot paper.
- Once each player has finished, begin Round 2 in which players make rectangles. Each round should be no more than 5 minutes.
- The pair with the most rectangles in all wins.

Other Ways to Play
- Have partners take turns making rectangles on their geoboard. Each rectangle should be hidden from the partner's view. The partner may ask only *yes* or *no* questions to try to make the same rectangle.
- **Challenge** Students who are familiar with the concept of perimeter can play a similar game in which they make polygons with given perimeters. Sample perimeters might include 8, 10, 12, and 14. Tell students that when they are making their polygons, they can only use vertical lines and horizontal lines. In this way, all of the units in the perimeters will be the same size. (The distance between two points on the geoboard is the same vertically and horizontally, but NOT diagonally.)

First-Place Math

Connecting Cubes

PARTNERS

Objective
- To use connecting cubes to explore using multiplication to find volume

Materials
- connecting cubes, paper, and pencil

> I have 2 layers of 4 rows of 6 blocks. How many blocks do I have in all?

> I have 4 layers of 2 rows of 3 blocks. How many blocks do I have in all?

Layers	Rows	In Each Row	Total
2	4	6	48
4	2	3	24

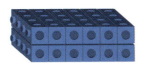

Riddle Me This

Get Ready
- Have each student make rectangular prisms with connecting cubes.
- Have each student use small pieces of paper to write at least 4 different riddles like the examples shown.

Let's Play
- Partners trade one riddle card.
- Each player uses connecting cubes to solve the riddle. He or she uses a recording sheet to describe the model.
- The partners trade models and recording sheets to check one another's work. Players score 1 point for a correct model and another point for a correct total.
- Play continues until all riddles are solved.

Other Ways to Play
- Have partners sit across from one another with a "wall" between them. Player A builds a rectangular prism and describes the prism to the other player. Player B builds an identical prism by listening to the description and then tells how many blocks were used in all.
- **Challenge** Players write riddles that are missing the number of layers, the number of rows, or the number in each row. Each riddle must give the total number of cubes used in the prism.

First-Place Math

Teaching Notes

Alternate Planners

3 WEEK PLANNERS
Week 1 . . . . .T184–T185
Week 2 . . . . .T186–T187
Week 3 . . . . .T188–T189

4 WEEK PLANNERS
Week 1 . . . . .T190–T191
Week 2 . . . . .T192–T193
Week 3 . . . . .T194–T195
Week 4 . . . . .T196–T197

5 WEEK PLANNERS
Week 1 . . . . .T198–T199
Week 2 . . . . .T200–T201
Week 3 . . . . .T202–T203
Week 4 . . . . .T204–T205
Week 5 . . . . .T206–T207

3-Week Plan
Week 1 Planner

OBJECTIVES
SKILLS
- To add 3- and 4-digit numbers
- To estimate sums to hundreds
- To subtract 3- and 4-digit numbers
- To subtract across zeros
- To multiply 2-, 3-, and 4-digit numbers by 1-digit numbers
- To multiply 2- and 3-digit numbers by 2-digit numbers
- To divide 2- and 3-digit numbers by 1-digit divisors
- To check division
- To divide 2- and 3-digit numbers by 2-digit divisors

	DAY 1 pages T4–T17, T31	**DAY 2** pages T18–T24
1 Warm-Up	**WARM-UP RESOURCES** Number of the Day, p. 1 Problem of the Day, p. 1 Quick Review, p. 1	**WARM-UP RESOURCES** Number of the Day, p. 4 Problem of the Day, p. 4 Quick Review, p. 4
2 Teach and Practice  	Adding 3-Digit Numbers, p. A1 Estimating Sums, p. A3 Adding 4-Digit Numbers, p. A4 Problem Solving, pp. A6–A7 3-Digit Subtraction, p. A8 Subtracting Across Zeros, p. A10 Use Estimation, p. A11 Make a Table, p. A12	Subtracting 4-Digit numbers, p. A13 Make a Graph, p. A15 Find a Pattern, p. A16 Add and Subtract, Start to Finish, p. A18
3 Extra Practice 	Fast Facts, p. P1 Use the Code, p. P2 Cross-number Puzzle, p. P3 Optional Pages pp. A2, A5, A9	What's Missing?, p. P4 The Sum of 1,089, p. P5 Facts Practice, p. P6 Optional Pages pp. A14, A17 Game: *Zoom*
4 Wrap Up and Assess 	**PRETEST** Book A Pretest, pp. 1–2 Book B Pretest, pp. 5–6	

T184 First-Place Math

OBJECTIVES (CONTINUED)
PROBLEM SOLVING
- To solve problems using estimation
- To solve problems by choosing the operation
- To identify what information is missing that is needed to solve a problem
- To find a pattern
- To solve problems by working backwards
- To solve problems using multiple steps
- To make a graph or table to solve problems

Book A
Addition and Subtraction

Book B
Multiplication and Division

DAY 3 pages T30, T32–T39	DAY 4 pages T40–T49	DAY 5 pages T25–T27, T50–T55
WARM-UP RESOURCES Number of the Day, p. 6 Problem of the Day, p. 6 Quick Review, p. 6	**WARM-UP RESOURCES** Number of the Day, p.8 Problem of the Day, p. 8 Quick Review, p. 8	**WARM-UP RESOURCES** Number of the Day, p. 10 Problem of the Day, p. 10 Quick Review, p. 10
Multiplying 2-Digit Numbers, p. B2 Multiplying 3-Digit Numbers, p. B3 Multiplying 4-Digit Numbers, p. B4 Work Backwards, p. B7	Multiplying 3-Digit Numbers, p. B8 Multi-Step Problems, p. B10 Dividing 2-Digit Numbers, p. B11 Dividing 3-Digit Numbers, p. B12 Checking Division, p. B14 Choose the Operation, p. B15	Dividing By 2-Digit Divisors, p. B16 Practice Multiplying and Dividing, p. B18
Alphabet Multiplication, p. P7 Practice Multiplying, p. P8 Optional Pages pp. B1, B5–B6	Missing Multiplication Digits, p. P9 Using Remainder Clues, p. P10 Optional Pages pp. B9, B13	Dividing by 2-Digit Divisors, p. P11 Facts Practice, p. P12 Optional Page p. B17 Game: *Zoom*
		WRAP UP Review, pp. A19 and B19 Home Connection, pp. A20 and B20 **TEST** Book A Test, pp. 3–4 Book B Test, pp. 7–8

Book A & B T185

3-Week Plan
Week 2 Planner

OBJECTIVES
SKILLS
- To find equivalent fractions
- To write fractions in simplest form
- To understand and write mixed numbers
- To add and subtract like fractions and mixed numbers
- To add and subtract unlike fractions using models
- To compare unlike fractions using models
- To compare and order decimals
- To add and subtract decimals
- To add and subtract money

	DAY 1 pages T58–T69, T91	DAY 2 pages T70–T81
1 Warm-Up	**WARM-UP RESOURCES** Number of the Day, p. 11 Problem of the Day, p. 11 Quick Review, p. 11	**WARM-UP RESOURCES** Number of the Day, p. 13 Problem of the Day, p. 13 Quick Review, p. 13
2 Teach and Practice 	Equivalent Fractions, pp. C1–C2 Simplest Form, p. C3 Mixed Numbers, pp. C5–C6 Adding Like Fractions, p. C7 Adding Like Mixed Numbers, p. C9 Make a Graph, p. C11	Subtracting Like Fractions, pp. C12–C13 Subtracting Like Mixed Numbers, p. C14 Choose the Operation, p. C16 Make a List, p. C17 Adding Unlike Fractions, p. C21 Subtracting Unlike Fractions, p. C22
3 Extra Practice 	Simplest Form, p. P13 Mixed Numbers, p. P14 Optional Pages pp. C4, C8, C10	It Makes a Difference!, p. P15 Fractions in Flight, p. P16 Optional Pages pp. C15, C18–C20, C23
4 Wrap Up and Assess 	**PRETEST** Book C Pretest, pp. 9–10 Book D Pretest, pp. 13–14	

T186 First-Place Math

OBJECTIVES (CONTINUED)
PROBLEM SOLVING

- To construct a bar graph to solve problems
- To solve problems by choosing the operation
- To make a list to solve problems
- To make a table to solve problems
- To determine when extra information is given in problems
- To determine when there is not enough information given to solve a problem
- To solve problems using multiple steps
- To solve problems using guess and check

Book C Fractions
Book D Decimals

DAY 3 pages T82–T85, T90, T92–T95	DAY 4 pages T96–T107	DAY 5 pages T86–T87, T108–T119
WARM-UP RESOURCES Number of the Day, p. 15 Problem of the Day, p. 15 Quick Review, p. 15	**WARM-UP RESOURCES** Number of the Day, p. 17 Problem of the Day, p. 17 Quick Review, p. 17	**WARM-UP RESOURCES** Number of the Day, p. 19 Problem of the Day, p. 19 Quick Review, p. 19
Comparing Unlike Fractions, p. C24 Finding Parts of Sets, p. C25 Equivalent Fractions, p. C26 Comparing and Ordering Decimals, p. D1 Adding Decimals, p. D3	Adding Decimals, pp. D5–D6 Extra Information, p. D9 Subtracting Decimals, pp. D11, D13 Make a Table, p. D15 Multi-Step Problems, p. D16	Subtracting Decimals, p. D18 Guess and Check, p. D20 Mixed Practice, p. D21 Adding and Subtracting Money, p. D24
Finding Parts of Sets, p. P17 Facts Practice, p. P18 Decimals Less Than 1, p. P19 Game: *Zoom* Optional Pages pp. D2, D4	Adding Decimals, p. P20 Subtracting Decimals, p. P21 Optional Pages pp. D7–D8, D10, D12, D14, D17	Count on, p. P22 Adding and Subtracting Money, p. P23 Facts Practice, p. P24 Game: *Hoop Time* Optional Pages pp. D19, D22–D23, D25–D26
		WRAP UP Review, pp. C27 and D27 Home Connection, pp. C28 and D28 **TEST** Book C Test, pp. 11–12 Book D Test, pp. 15–16

3-Week Plan

Week 3 Planner

OBJECTIVES
SKILLS
- To identify plane and solid figures
- To identify and name points, lines, and segments
- To identify parallel lines and intersecting lines
- To identify rays and angles, including right angles
- To identify congruent shapes and similar figures
- To identify lines of symmetry
- To identify and use ordered pairs
- To tell and estimate time; to understand temperature
- To measure objects to the nearest $\frac{1}{2}$ and $\frac{1}{4}$ inch

	DAY 1 pages T122–T133, T149	**DAY 2** pages T134–T142
1 Warm-Up	**WARM-UP RESOURCES** Number of the Day, p. 21 Problem of the Day, p. 21 Quick Review, p. 21	**WARM-UP RESOURCES** Number of the Day, p. 24 Problem of the Day, p. 24 Quick Review, p. 24
2 Teach and Practice  	Plane and Solid Figures, pp. E1–E2 Points, Lines, and Segments, p. E3 Parallel and Intersecting Lines, p. E4 Rays and Angles, p. E5 Multi-Step Problems, p. E6 Right Angles, p. E7 Find a Pattern, p. E8	Congruent Figures, p. E11 Similar Figures, p. E13 Lines of Symmetry, p. E15 Use Logic, pp. E16–E17 Ordered Pairs, p. E18
3 Extra Practice 	Figure Faces, p. P25 Rays and Angles, p. P26 Right Angle Search, p. P27 Optional Pages pp. E9–E10	Lines of Symmetry, p. P28 Ordered Pairs, p. P29 Facts Practice, p. P30 Optional Pages pp. E12, E14 Game: *Hoop Time*
4 Wrap Up and Assess 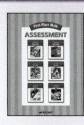	**PRETEST** Book E Pretest, pp. 17–18 Book F Pretest, pp. 21–22	

T188 First-Place Math

OBJECTIVES (CONTINUED)

SKILLS (CONTINUED)
- To estimate length, capacity, and weight in customary and metric units
- To find the perimeter, area, and volume of objects

PROBLEM SOLVING
- To solve problems using multiple steps
- To find a pattern
- To use logic to solve problems
- To solve problems by making lists

Book E Geometry
Book F Measurement

DAY 3
pages T148–T159

WARM-UP RESOURCES
Number of the Day, p. 26
Problem of the Day, p. 26
Quick Review, p. 26

Time, pp. F1–F3
Elapsed Time, p. F4
Degrees Fahrenheit and Celsius, pp. F6–F7
Fractions of an Inch, p. F8
Measuring Millimeters and Centimeters, p. F11
Multi-Step Problems, p. F13

Telling Time, p. P31
Measuring Millimeters and Centimeters, p. P32
Optional Pages pp. F5, F9–F10, F12

DAY 4
pages T160–T169

WARM-UP RESOURCES
Number of the Day, p. 28
Problem of the Day, p. 28
Quick Review, p. 28

Perimeter, p. F14
Area, pp. F15–F16
Make a List, p. F17
Cup, Pint, Quart, and Gallon, p. F18
Estimating Milliliters and Liters, p. F20
Volume, p. F22
Guess and Check, p. F24

Area, p. P33
Perimeter, p. P34

Optional Pages pp. F19, F21, F23

DAY 5
pages T143–T145, T170–T175

WARM-UP RESOURCES
Number of the Day, p.30
Problem of the Day, p. 30
Quick Review, p. 30

Estimating Ounces, Pounds, and Tons, p. F25
Estimating Grams and Kilograms, p. F26

Estimating Ounces, Pounds, and Tons, p. P35

Game: *Hoop Time*

WRAP UP
Review, pp. E19 and F27
Home Connection, pp. E20 and F28

TEST
Book E Test, pp. 19–20
Book F Test, pp. 23–24

Book E & F T189

4-Week Plan

Week 1 Planner

OBJECTIVES

SKILLS
- To add 3-digit and 4-digit numbers
- To estimate sums to hundreds
- To subtract 3-digit and 4-digit numbers
- To subtract across zeros
- To practice addition and subtraction

	DAY 1 pages T4–T7	**DAY 2** pages T8–T11
1 Warm-Up 	**WARM-UP RESOURCES** Number of the Day, p. 1 Problem of the Day, p. 1 Quick Review, p. 1	**WARM-UP RESOURCES** Number of the Day, p. 2 Problem of the Day, p. 2 Quick Review, p. 2
2 Teach and Practice 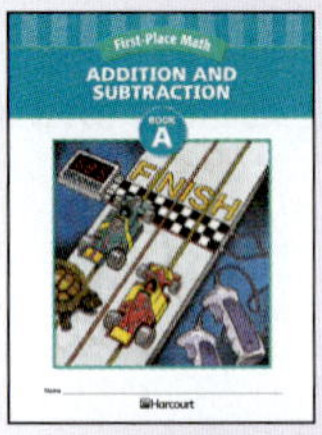	Adding 3-Digit Numbers, p. A1 More Addition, p. A2	Estimating Sums to the Hundreds, p. A3 Adding 4-Digit Numbers, pp. A4–A5 Choose the Operation, p. A6 Too Little Information, p. A7
3 Extra Practice 	Fast Facts, p. P1	Use the Code, p. P2
4 Wrap Up and Assess 	**PRETEST** Book A Pretest, pp. 1–2 Assess knowledge of addition, subtraction, and problem solving	

First-Place Math

Addition and Subtraction

OBJECTIVES (CONTINUED)
PROBLEM SOLVING
- To solve problems by choosing the operation
- To identify what information is missing that is needed to solve a problem
- To solve problems using estimation
- To make a table to solve problems
- To make a graph to solve problems
- To find a pattern

DAY 3
pages T12–T17

WARM-UP RESOURCES
Number of the Day, p. 3
Problem of the Day, p. 3
Quick Review, p. 3

3-Digit Subtraction, p. A8
Subtracting 3-Digit Numbers, p. A9
Subtracting Across Zeros, p. A10
Use Estimation, p. A11
Make a Table, p. A12

Cross-number Puzzle, p. P3

DAY 4
pages T18–T21

WARM-UP RESOURCES
Number of the Day, p. 4
Problem of the Day, p. 4
Quick Review, p. 4

Subtracting 4-Digit Numbers, p. A13
Practice Adding and Subtracting, p. A14
Make a Graph, p. A15
Find a Pattern, p. A16

What's Missing?, p. P4

DAY 5
pages T22–T27

WARM-UP RESOURCES
Number of the Day, p. 5
Problem of the Day, p. 5
Quick Review, p. 5

Practice Adding and Subtracting, p. A17
Add and Subtract, Start to Finish, p. A18

The Sum of 1,089, p. P5
Facts Practice, p. P6

Game: *Zoom*

WRAP UP
Review, p. A19
Home Connection, p. A20

TEST
Book A Test, pp. 3–4
    Assess knowledge of addition, subtraction, and problem solving

Book A   T191

4-Week Plan

Week 2 Planner

OBJECTIVES

SKILLS

- To multiply 2-, 3-, and 4-digit numbers by 1-digit numbers
- To multiply 2- and 3-digit numbers by 2-digit numbers
- To divide 2- and 3-digit numbers by 1-digit divisors
- To check division
- To divide 2- and 3-digit numbers by 2-digit divisors

	DAY 1 pages T30–T35	**DAY 2** pages T36–T39
1 Warm-Up	**WARM-UP RESOURCES** Number of the Day, p. 6 Problem of the Day, p. 6 Quick Review, p. 6	**WARM-UP RESOURCES** Number of the Day, p. 7 Problem of the Day, p. 7 Quick Review, p. 7
2 Teach and Practice	Facts Practice, p. B1 Multiplying 2-Digit Numbers, p. B2 Multiplying 3-Digit Numbers, p. B3 Multiplying 4-Digit Numbers, p. B4	Multiplying 2-Digit Numbers, pp. B5–B6 Work Backwards, p. B7
3 Extra Practice	Alphabet Multiplication, p. P7	Practice Multiplying, p. P8
4 Wrap Up and Assess	**PRETEST** Book B Pretest, pp. 5–6 Assess knowledge of multiplication, division, and problem solving	

First-Place Math

Multiplication and Division

OBJECTIVES (CONTINUED)
PROBLEM SOLVING
- To solve problems by working backwards
- To solve problems using multiple steps
- To solve problems by choosing the operation

DAY 3 pages T40–T43	**DAY 4** pages T44–T49	**DAY 5** pages T50–T55
WARM-UP RESOURCES Number of the Day, p. 8 Problem of the Day, p. 8 Quick Review, p. 8	**WARM-UP RESOURCES** Number of the Day, p. 9 Problem of the Day, p. 9 Quick Review, p. 9	**WARM-UP RESOURCES** Number of the Day, p. 10 Problem of the Day, p. 10 Quick Review, p. 10
Multiplying 3-Digit Numbers, pp. B8–B9 Multi-Step Problems, p. B10	Dividing 2-Digit Numbers, p. B11 Dividing 3-Digit Numbers, pp. B12–B13 Checking Division, p. B14 Choose the Operation, p. B15	Dividing by 2-Digit Divisors, pp. B16–B17 Practice Multiplying and Dividing, p. B18
Missing Multiplication Digits, p. P9	Using Remainder Clues, p. P10	Dividing by 2-Digit Divisors, p. P11 Facts Practice, p. P12 Game: *Zoom*
		WRAP UP Review, p. B19 Home Connection, p. B20 **TEST** Book B Test, pp. 7–8 Assess knowledge of multiplication, division, and problem solving

Book B

4-Week Plan

Week 3 Planner

OBJECTIVES
SKILLS
- To find equivalent fractions
- To write fractions in simplest form
- To understand and write mixed numbers
- To add and subtract like fractions and mixed numbers
- To add and subtract unlike fractions using models
- To compare unlike fractions using models
- To compare and order decimals
- To add and subtract decimals
- To add and subtract money

	DAY 1 pages T58–T69, T91	**DAY 2** pages T70–T81
1 Warm-Up	**WARM-UP RESOURCES** Number of the Day, p. 11 Problem of the Day, p. 11 Quick Review, p. 11	**WARM-UP RESOURCES** Number of the Day, p. 13 Problem of the Day, p. 13 Quick Review, p. 13
2 Teach and Practice 	Equivalent Fractions, pp. C1–C2 Simplest Form, p. C3 Mixed Numbers, pp. C5–C6 Adding Like Fractions, p. C7 Adding Like Mixed Numbers, p. C9 Make a Graph, p. C11	Subtracting Like Fractions, pp. C12–C13 Subtracting Like Mixed Numbers, p. C4 Choose the Operation, p. C16 Make a List, p. C17 Adding Unlike Fractions, p. C21 Subtracting Unlike Fractions, p. C22
3 Extra Practice 	Simplest Form, p. P13 Mixed Numbers, p. P14 Optional Pages pp. C4, C8, C10	It Makes a Difference!, p. P15 Fractions in Flight, p. P16 Optional Pages pp. C15, C18–C20, C23
4 Wrap Up and Assess 	**PRETEST** Book C Pretest, pp. 9–10 Book D Pretest, pp. 13–14	

T194 First-Place Math

OBJECTIVES (CONTINUED)
PROBLEM SOLVING
- To construct a bar graph to solve problems
- To solve problems by choosing the operation
- To make a list to solve problems
- To make a table to solve problems
- To determine when extra information is given in problems
- To determine when there is not enough information given to solve a problem
- To solve problems using multiple steps
- To solve problems using guess and check

Book C Fractions
Book D Decimals

DAY 3 pages T82–T85, T90, T92–T95	DAY 4 pages T96–T107	DAY 5 pages T86–T87, T108–T119
WARM-UP RESOURCES Number of the Day, p. 15 Problem of the Day, p. 15 Quick Review, p. 15	**WARM-UP RESOURCES** Number of the Day, p. 17 Problem of the Day, p. 17 Quick Review, p. 17	**WARM-UP RESOURCES** Number of the Day, p. 19 Problem of the Day, p. 19 Quick Review, p. 19
Comparing Unlike Fractions, p. C24 Finding Parts of Sets, p. C25 Equivalent Fractions, p. C26 Comparing and Ordering Decimals, p. D1 Adding Decimals, p. D3	Adding Decimals, pp. D5–D6 Extra Information, p. D9 Subtracting Decimals, pp. D11, D13 Make a Table, p. D15 Multi-Step Problems, p. D16	Subtracting Decimals, p. D18 Guess and Check, p. D20 Mixed Practice, p. D21 Adding and Subtracting Money, p. D24
Finding Parts of Sets, p. P17 Facts Practice, p. P18 Decimals Less Than 1, p. P19 Game: *Zoom* Optional Pages pp. D2, D4	Adding Decimals, p. P20 Subtracting Decimals, p. P21 Optional Pages pp. D7–D8, D10, D12, D14, D17	Count on, p. P22 Adding and Subtracting Money, p. P23 Facts Practice, p. P24 Game: *Hoop Time* Optional Pages pp. D19, D22–D23, D25–D26
		WRAP UP Review, pp. C27 and D27 Home Connection, pp. C28 and D28 **TEST** Book C Test, pp. 11–12 Book D Test, pp. 15–16

Book C & D T195

4-Week Plan
Week 4 Planner

OBJECTIVES
SKILLS
- To identify plane and solid figures
- To identify and name points, lines, and segments
- To identify parallel lines and intersecting lines
- To identify rays and angles, including right angles
- To identify congruent shapes and similar figures
- To identify lines of symmetry
- To identify and use ordered pairs
- To tell and estimate time; to understand temperature
- To measure objects to the nearest $\frac{1}{2}$ and $\frac{1}{4}$ inch

	DAY 1 pages T122–T133, T149	**DAY 2** pages T134–T142
1 Warm-Up	**WARM-UP RESOURCES** Number of the Day, p. 21 Problem of the Day, p. 21 Quick Review, p. 21	**WARM-UP RESOURCES** Number of the Day, p. 24 Problem of the Day, p. 24 Quick Review, p. 24
2 Teach and Practice 	Plane and Solid Figures, pp. E1–E2 Points, Lines, and Segments, p. E3 Parallel and Intersecting Lines, p. E4 Rays and Angles, p. E5 Multi-Step Problems, p. E6 Right Angles, p. E7 Find a Pattern, p. E8	Congruent Figures, p. E11 Similar Figures, p. E13 Lines of Symmetry, p. E15 Use Logic, pp. E16–E17 Ordered Pairs, p. E18
3 Extra Practice 	Figure Faces, p. P25 Rays and Angles, p. P26 Right Angle Search, p. P27 Optional Pages pp. E9–E10	Lines of Symmetry, p. P28 Ordered Pairs, p. P29 Facts Practice, p. P30 Optional Pages pp. E12, E14 Game: *Hoop Time*
4 Wrap Up and Assess 	**PRETEST** Book E Pretest, pp. 17–18 Book F Pretest, pp. 21–22	

T196 First-Place Math

OBJECTIVES (CONTINUED)

SKILLS (CONTINUED)
- To estimate length, capacity, and weight in customary and metric units
- To find the perimeter, area, and volume of objects

PROBLEM SOLVING
- To solve problems using multiple steps
- To find a pattern
- To use logic to solve problems
- To solve problems by making lists

DAY 3 pages T148–T159	DAY 4 pages T160–T169	DAY 5 pages T143–T145, T170–T175
WARM-UP RESOURCES Number of the Day, p. 26 Problem of the Day, p. 26 Quick Review, p. 26	**WARM-UP RESOURCES** Number of the Day, p. 28 Problem of the Day, p. 28 Quick Review, p. 28	**WARM-UP RESOURCES** Number of the Day, p.30 Problem of the Day, p. 30 Quick Review, p. 30
Time, pp. F1–F3 Elapsed Time, p. F4 Degrees Fahrenheit and Celsius, pp. F6–F7 Fractions of an Inch, p. F8 Measuring Millimeters and Centimeters, p. F11 Multi-Step Problems, p. F13	Perimeter, p. F14 Area, pp. F15–F16 Make a List, p. F17 Cup, Pint, Quart, and Gallon, p. F18 Estimating Milliliters and Liters, p. F20 Volume, p. F22 Guess and Check, p. F24	Estimating Ounces, Pounds, and Tons, p. F25 Estimating Grams and Kilograms, p. F26
Telling Time, p. P31 Measuring Millimeters and Centimeters, p. P32 Optional Pages pp. F5, F9–F10, F12	Area, p. P33 Perimeter, p. P34 Optional Pages pp. F19, F21, F23	Estimating Ounces, Pounds, and Tons, p. P35 Game: *Hoop Time*
		WRAP UP Review, pp. E19 and F27 Home Connection, pp. E20 and F28 **TEST** Book E Test, pp. 19–20 Book F Test, pp. 23–24

Book E & F T197

Week 1 Planner

OBJECTIVES
SKILLS
- To add 3-digit and 4-digit numbers
- To estimate sums to hundreds
- To subtract 3-digit and 4-digit numbers
- To subtract across zeros
- To practice addition and subtraction

	DAY 1 pages T4–T7	**DAY 2** pages T8–T11
1 Warm-Up	**WARM-UP RESOURCES** Number of the Day, p. 1 Problem of the Day, p. 1 Quick Review, p. 1	**WARM-UP RESOURCES** Number of the Day, p. 2 Problem of the Day, p. 2 Quick Review, p. 2
2 Teach and Practice	Adding 3-Digit Numbers, p. A1 More Addition, p. A2	Estimating Sums to the Hundreds, p. A3 Adding 4-Digit Numbers, pp. A4–A5 Choose the Operation, p. A6 Too Little Information, p. A7
3 Extra Practice	Fast Facts, p. P1	Use the Code, p. P2
4 Wrap Up and Assess	**PRETEST** Book A Pretest, pp. 1–2 Assess knowledge of addition, subtraction, and problem solving	

T198 First-Place Math

Addition and Subtraction

OBJECTIVES (CONTINUED)
PROBLEM SOLVING

- To solve problems by choosing the operation
- To identify what information is missing that is needed to solve a problem
- To solve problems using estimation
- To make a table to solve problems
- To make a graph to solve problems
- To find a pattern

DAY 3 pages T12–T17	DAY 4 pages T18–T21	DAY 5 pages T22–T27
WARM-UP RESOURCES Number of the Day, p. 3 Problem of the Day, p. 3 Quick Review, p. 3	**WARM-UP RESOURCES** Number of the Day, p. 4 Problem of the Day, p. 4 Quick Review, p. 4	**WARM-UP RESOURCES** Number of the Day, p. 5 Problem of the Day, p. 5 Quick Review, p. 5
3-Digit Subtraction, p. A8 Subtracting 3-Digit Numbers, p. A9 Subtracting Across Zeros, p. A10 Use Estimation, p. A11 Make a Table, p. A12	Subtracting 4-Digit Numbers, p. A13 Practice Adding and Subtracting, p. A14 Make a Graph, p. A15 Find a Pattern, p. A16	Practice Adding and Subtracting, p. A17 Add and Subtract, Start to Finish, p. A18
Cross-number Puzzle, p. P3	What's Missing?, p. P4	The Sum of 1,089, p. P5 Facts Practice, p. P6 Game: *Zoom*
		WRAP UP Review, p. A19 Home Connection, p. A20 **TEST** Book A Test, pp. 3–4 Assess knowledge of addition, subtraction, and problem solving

Book A T199

5-Week Plan

Week 2 Planner

OBJECTIVES
SKILLS
- To multiply 2-, 3-, and 4-digit numbers by 1-digit numbers
- To multiply 2- and 3-digit numbers by 2-digit numbers
- To divide 2- and 3-digit numbers by 1-digit divisors
- To check division
- To divide 2- and 3-digit numbers by 2-digit divisors

	DAY 1 pages T30–T35	**DAY 2** pages T36–T39
1 Warm-Up 	**WARM-UP RESOURCES** Number of the Day, p. 6 Problem of the Day, p. 6 Quick Review, p. 6	**WARM-UP RESOURCES** Number of the Day, p. 7 Problem of the Day, p. 7 Quick Review, p. 7
2 Teach and Practice 	Facts Practice, p. B1 Multiplying 2-Digit Numbers, p. B2 Multiplying 3-Digit Numbers, p. B3 Multiplying 4-Digit Numbers, p. B4	Multiplying 2-Digit Numbers, pp. B5–B6 Work Backwards, p. B7
3 Extra Practice 	Alphabet Multiplication, p. P7	Practice Multiplying, p. P8
4 Wrap Up and Assess 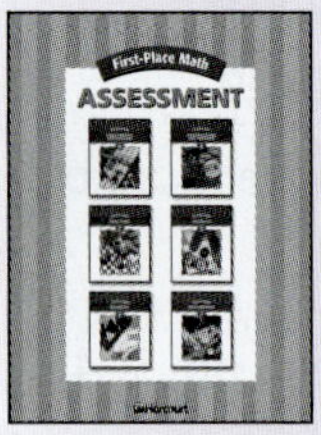	**PRETEST** Book B Pretest, pp. 5–6 Assess knowledge of multiplication, division, and problem solving	

First-Place Math

OBJECTIVES (CONTINUED)
PROBLEM SOLVING
- To solve problems by working backwards
- To solve problems using multiple steps
- To solve problems by choosing the operation

Multiplication and Division

DAY 3 pages T40–T43	**DAY 4** pages T44–T49	**DAY 5** pages T50–T55
WARM-UP RESOURCES Number of the Day, p. 8 Problem of the Day, p. 8 Quick Review, p. 8	**WARM-UP RESOURCES** Number of the Day, p. 9 Problem of the Day, p. 9 Quick Review, p. 9	**WARM-UP RESOURCES** Number of the Day, p. 10 Problem of the Day, p. 10 Quick Review, p. 10
Multiplying 3-Digit Numbers, pp. B8–B9 Multi-Step Problems, p. B10	Dividing 2-Digit Numbers, p. B11 Dividing 3-Digit Numbers, pp. B12–B13 Checking Division, p. B14 Choose the Operation, p. B15	Dividing by 2-Digit Divisors, pp. B16–B17 Practice Multiplying and Dividing, p. B18
Missing Multiplication Digits, p. P9	Using Remainder Clues, p. P10	Dividing by 2-Digit Divisors, p. P11 Facts Practice, p. P12 Game: *Zoom*
		WRAP UP Review, p. B19 Home Connection, p. B20 **TEST** Book B Test, pp. 7–8 Assess knowledge of multiplication, division, and problem solving

Book B T201

5-Week Plan

Week 3 Planner

OBJECTIVES
SKILLS
- To find equivalent fractions
- To write fractions in simplest form
- To understand and write mixed numbers
- To add and subtract like fractions and express answers in simplest form
- To add and subtract mixed numbers
- To add and subtract like mixed numbers and record the answer in simplest form
- To add and subtract unlike fractions using models

	DAY 1 pages T58–T63	**DAY 2** pages T64–T69
1 Warm-Up	**WARM-UP RESOURCES** Number of the Day, p. 11 Problem of the Day, p. 11 Quick Review, p. 11	**WARM-UP RESOURCES** Number of the Day, p. 12 Problem of the Day, p. 12 Quick Review, p. 12
2 Teach and Practice 	Equivalent Fractions, pp. C1–C2, Simplest Form, pp. C3–C4	Mixed Numbers, pp. C5–C6 Adding Like Fractions, pp. C7–C8 Adding Like Mixed Numbers, p. C9 Extra Information, p. C10 Make a Graph, p. C11
3 Extra Practice 	Simplest Form, p. P13	Mixed Numbers, p. P14
4 Wrap Up and Assess 	**PRETEST** Book C Pretest, pp. 9–10 Assess knowledge of fractions and problem solving	

T202 First-Place Math

Fractions

OBJECTIVES (CONTINUED)

SKILLS (CONTINUED)
- To compare unlike fractions
- To find part of a set for a given fraction

PROBLEM SOLVING
- To determine when extra information is given in problems
- To construct a bar graph to solve problems
- To solve problems by choosing the operation
- To make a list to solve problems
- To solve problems by working backwards

DAY 3 pages T70–T75	DAY 4 pages T76–T81	DAY 5 pages T82–T87
WARM-UP RESOURCES Number of the Day, p. 13 Problem of the Day, p. 13 Quick Review, p. 13	**WARM-UP RESOURCES** Number of the Day, p. 14 Problem of the Day, p. 14 Quick Review, p. 14	**WARM-UP RESOURCES** Number of the Day, p. 15 Problem of the Day, p. 15 Quick Review, p. 15
Subtracting Like Fractions, pp. C12–C13 Subtracting Like Mixed Numbers, p. C14 Adding and Subtracting Mixed Numbers, p. C15 Choose the Operation, p. C16 Make a List, p. C17	Adding Like Mixed Numbers, p. C18 Subtracting Like Mixed Numbers, p. C19 Adding and Subtracting Mixed Numbers, p. C20 Adding Unlike Fractions, p. C21 Subtracting Unlike Fractions, p. C22 Work Backwards, p. C23	Comparing Unlike Fractions, p. C24 Finding Parts of Sets, p. C25 Equivalent Fractions, p. C26
It Makes a Difference!, p. P15	Fractions in Flight, p. P16	Finding Parts of Sets, p. P17 Facts Practice, p. P18  Game: *Zoom*
		WRAP UP Review, p. C27 Home Connection, p. C28 **TEST** Book C Test, pp. 11–12 Assess knowledge of fractions and problem solving

Book C T203

5-Week Plan
Week 4 Planner

OBJECTIVES
SKILLS
- To compare and order decimals
- To add decimals
- To subtract decimals
- To add and subtract decimals to hundredths
- To add and subtract money

	DAY 1 pages T90–T95	**DAY 2** pages T96–T101
1 Warm-Up	**WARM-UP RESOURCES** Number of the Day, p. 16 Problem of the Day, p. 16 Quick Review, p. 16	**WARM-UP RESOURCES** Number of the Day, p. 17 Problem of the Day, p. 17 Quick Review, p. 17
2 Teach and Practice	Comparing and Ordering Decimals, pp. D1–D2 Adding Decimals, pp. D3–D4	Adding Decimals, pp. D5–D8 Extra Information, p. D9 Too Little Information, p. D10
3 Extra Practice	Decimals Less Than 1, p. P19	Adding Decimals, p. P20
4 Wrap Up and Assess	**PRETEST** Book D Pretest, pp. 13–14 Assess knowledge of decimals and problem solving	

First-Place Math

Decimals

OBJECTIVES (CONTINUED)
PROBLEM SOLVING
- To determine when extra information is given in problems
- To determine when there is not enough information given to solve a problem
- To make a table to solve problems
- To solve problems using multiple steps
- To solve problems using guess and check

DAY 3
pages T102–T107

WARM-UP RESOURCES
Number of the Day, p. 18
Problem of the Day, p. 18
Quick Review, p. 18

Subtracting Decimals, pp. D11–D14
Make a Table, p. D15
Multi-Step Problems, p. D16
Mixed Practice, p. D17

Subtracting Decimals, p. P21

DAY 4
pages T108–T113

WARM-UP RESOURCES
Number of the Day, p. 19
Problem of the Day, p. 19
Quick Review, p. 19

Subtracting Decimals, pp. D18–D19
Guess and Check, p. D20
Mixed Practice, pp. D21–D23

Count On, p. P22

DAY 5
pages T114–T119

WARM-UP RESOURCES
Number of the Day, p. 20
Problem of the Day, p. 20
Quick Review, p. 20

Adding and Subtracting Money, pp. D24–D26

Adding and Subtracting Money, p. P23
Facts Practice, p. P24

Game: *Hoop Time*

WRAP UP
Review, p. D27
Home Connection, p. D28

TEST
Book D Test, pp. 15–16
   Assess knowledge of decimals and problem solving

Book D T205

5-Week Plan

Week 5 Planner

OBJECTIVES
SKILLS
- To identify plane and solid figures
- To identify and name points, lines, and segments
- To identify parallel lines and intersecting lines
- To identify rays and angles, including right angles
- To identify congruent shapes and similar figures
- To identify lines of symmetry
- To identify and use ordered pairs
- To tell and estimate time; to understand temperature
- To measure objects to the nearest $\frac{1}{2}$ and $\frac{1}{4}$ inch

	DAY 1 pages T122–T133, T149	**DAY 2** pages T134–T142
1 Warm-Up	**WARM-UP RESOURCES** Number of the Day, p. 21 Problem of the Day, p. 21 Quick Review, p. 21	**WARM-UP RESOURCES** Number of the Day, p. 24 Problem of the Day, p. 24 Quick Review, p. 24
2 Teach and Practice 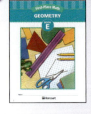	Plane and Solid Figures, pp. E1–E2 Points, Lines, and Segments, p. E3 Parallel and Intersecting Lines, p. E4 Rays and Angles, p. E5 Multi-Step Problems, p. E6 Right Angles, p. E7 Find a Pattern, p. E8	Congruent Figures, p. E11 Similar Figures, p. E13 Lines of Symmetry, p. E15 Use Logic, pp. E16–E17 Ordered Pairs, p. E18
3 Extra Practice 	Figure Faces, p. P25 Rays and Angles, p. P26 Right Angle Search, p. P27 Optional Pages pp. E9–E10	Lines of Symmetry, p. P28 Ordered Pairs, p. P29 Facts Practice, p. P30 Optional Pages pp. E12, E14 Game: *Hoop Time*
4 Wrap Up and Assess 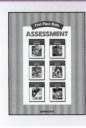	**PRETEST** Book E Pretest, pp. 17–18 Book F Pretest, pp. 21–22	

First-Place Math

OBJECTIVES (CONTINUED)

SKILLS (CONTINUED)
- To estimate length, capacity, and weight in customary and metric units
- To find the perimeter, area, and volume of objects

PROBLEM SOLVING
- To solve problems using multiple steps
- To find a pattern
- To use logic to solve problems
- To solve problems by making lists

Book E Geometry
Book F Measurement

DAY 3 pages T148–T159	**DAY 4** pages T160–T169	**DAY 5** pages T143–T145, T170–T175
WARM-UP RESOURCES Number of the Day, p. 26 Problem of the Day, p. 26 Quick Review, p. 26	**WARM-UP RESOURCES** Number of the Day, p. 28 Problem of the Day, p. 28 Quick Review, p. 28	**WARM-UP RESOURCES** Number of the Day, p. 30 Problem of the Day, p. 30 Quick Review, p. 30
Time, pp. F1–F3 Elapsed Time, p. F4 Degrees Fahrenheit and Celsius, pp. F6–F7 Fractions of an Inch, p. F8 Measuring Millimeters and Centimeters, p. F11 Multi-Step Problems, p. F13	Perimeter, p. F14 Area, pp. F15–F16 Make a List, p. F17 Cup, Pint, Quart, and Gallon, p. F18 Estimating Milliliters and Liters, p. F20 Volume, p. F22 Guess and Check, p. F24	Estimating Ounces, Pounds, and Tons, p. F25 Estimating Grams and Kilograms, p. F26
Telling Time, p. P31 Measuring Millimeters and Centimeters, p. P32 Optional Pages pp. F5, F9–F10, F12	Area, p. P33 Perimeter, p. P34 Optional Pages pp. F19, F21, F23	Estimating Ounces, Pounds, and Tons, p. P35 Game: *Hoop Time*
		WRAP UP Review, pp. E19 and F27 Home Connection, pp. E20 and F28 **TEST** Book E Test, pp. 19–20 Book F Test, pp. 23–24